SURROGATE TERRORISTS

Iran's Formula for Success

Stephen Kramer

University Press of America,® Inc.
Lanham · Boulder · New York · Toronto · Plymouth, UK

Library of Congress Control Number: 2009943115
ISBN: 978-0-7618-5068-7 (paperback : alk. paper)

Contents

"We shall export our revolution to the whole world."

Ayatollah Khomeini*

---

* Robin Wright, *Sacred Rage: The Wrath of Militant Islam* (New York: Simon and Schuster, 1985), 27.

Preface

The goal of this preface is to guide all readers of this book toward a common understanding of certain necessary concepts, terms, and definitions. While there are many definitions of certain terms and many discussions about the following topics, what follows could be viewed as common ground. Certainly, there is still some room for disagreement. But hopefully the following information regarding militias, insurgencies, terrorism, as well as a brief discussion on analytic methodologies and the practice of denial and deception, will help the reader to better understand the information about Hizballah, Iran, the Lebanese Civil War, and all topics presented in this book.

Militiaman, Insurgent, or Terrorist

Militia

A militia can be viewed as a group of local citizens who are acting in their community's best interest by providing civil order when the government is unable or unwilling to provide this fundamental service. Militias are formed to safeguard villages, tribes, or sectarian groups. They are "often considered legitimate entities acting morally in the absence of effective national, provincial, or local security institutions." They "function to protect neighborhoods and meet the socio-economic needs of their limited constituency."[1] They are not just security forces; they act to aid the community in obtaining basic social needs as well.

Militias swear allegiance to non-nationalistic entities such as tribal leaders because the government is not in a position powerful enough to provide leadership in a community backed by force. They are, hopefully, an interim solution to quell violence until national security forces are able to provide decisive security.[2]

Generally speaking, militias do not attack occupying forces or what limited forces the weak government can provide. A good example of this is the Kurdish Peshmerga of northern Iraq. They have been an unauthorized armed force supported by a legitimate Kurdish Regional Government.[3] Militias that conduct themselves as a somewhat professional armed force are sometimes asked to join a strengthening government security force or army rather than laying down their arms. However, this amnesty may be extended out of practicality, as a fledgling government often does not have the resources to forcibly disarm a seasoned and battle-hardened militia.

Militias do not always work in alliance with an occupying force or weak central government's security force. The Badr Corps, the paramilitary wing of the politically powerful Supreme Council for the Islamic Revolution in Iraq, and Muqtada as-Sadr's Jaysh al-Mahdi have often battled Coalition Forces and Iraqi security forces in Baghdad since the US-Coalition invasion in 2003.

On the negative side, while militias often provide much needed security, their allegiances do not necessarily extend to the state. They often remain loyal to their militia leaders even after the state has proven that it can resume the role of protectors of the populace. Militias receive funds from foreign supporters, collection of border taxes, and provision of private security. These careers are often more lucrative and more stable than what the new government can offer. Therefore it is difficult to convince a successful and prosperous militia to support state-sponsored initiatives or, at the least, step aside and let the state take control.[4]

Insurgency

An insurgency can be defined as "a violent competition between a state and a rival political group to control a population or establish an alternate political order."[5] It is not only a military struggle but also a political struggle "by an organized movement seeking to subvert or displace the government and completely or partially control the resources and population of a country through the use of force and alternative political organizations." As stated in the US State Department's Bureau of Political-Military Affairs 2007 publication *Counterinsurgency for U.S. Government Policy Makers: A Work in Progress*, the insurgents' intent is to control a particular area or population and its resources.[6]

A weak state does not have to already exist in order for an insurgency to form. The insurgent's goal is to weaken government control over an area and destroy the government's legitimacy as a responsible and just governing body. As stated in the RAND study "War by Other Means: Building Complete and Balanced Capabilities for Counterinsurgency" by David C. Gompert and John Gordon IV, the insurgents "have an alternative vision of how to organize society, and they use various instruments, ranging from public service to terror, to realize that vision."7

Strategy and tactics employed by insurgents have changed since the heyday of revolutionary warfare in the 1950s and 1960s. The classic insurgency model is based on the concepts of Mao Tse-Tung and revolutionary warfare.8

Classic Insurgency—Mao Tse-Tung

Mao Tse-Tung led the Chinese Communists in the Civil War in China in the first half of the twentieth century. His strategy of the People's War inspired many revolutionary insurgencies in the years that followed. This classic insurgency usually pitted an internal non-state actor against a single, host government.

Mao's insurgency strategy was to build the movement step-by-step culminating in the revolutionary movement seizing control over the state and replacing it with a government of its own design based on its revolutionary principles. The insurgency begins with intensive underground political activities to build a base of support. From this base of support were drawn guerrilla fighters that would target local governments in order to destroy their control over the population and create a power vacuum in that area. The mobilization of the populace against the regime is a critical factor. "Without the support of the majority of the populace, the revolutionaries would remain too weak to defeat the regime and its instruments of coercion."9 The insurgents are extremely weak compared to the regime at this stage. It is therefore important to avoid the overwhelming force of the government. In this phase terrorist tactics enjoy their greatest relative utility.

The insurgents would then move into the area now deprived of government support and slowly expand. The primary military objective in this phase is to secure "liberated" zones in which bases for recruitment and training can be built. The insurgents will then begin to attack the regime's forces directly while avoiding excessive losses. The insurgency cannot move into this phase if it is not prepared to rely less on terrorism and more on guerrilla warfare.[10] Eventually, when the movement had enough popular support and the guerrilla forces were militarily strong enough, the government forces would be defeated in conventional engagements.[11]

The classic guerrilla insurgency grew in the sanctuary of the outlying countryside far from the government's urban centers of power. The insurgents were protected by distance and complex terrain such as mountains, dense forest, and wild jungle. These settings offered "sanctuary for insurgent forces to train and rest. They also afforded the insurgent cover, protection, and sustenance required." It wasn't until later in the conflict when the guerrillas were strong enough that they moved into the urban areas to defeat the government forces in decisive battles.[12]

Effective revolutionary movements based on Mao's strategy were very well organized and centrally controlled. A good example was the Viet Cong of the Vietnam War.

> at the head of the Viet Cong was the Central Office for South Vietnam (COSVN), a committee composed of top political and military leaders. Below the COSVN were six regional committees, each of which oversaw several provincial and district offices. At the district level was an extensive support organization including medical personnel, weapons manufacturers, training teams, and fiscal auditors. At the lowest level, the cadre organized the entire population to support the movement. Armed bodies consisted of main force units, local guerrillas, and village militias. These military units were fully integrated with the political hierarchy, giving the Viet Cong tight organizational control.[13]

Modern Insurgency

The modern insurgent is different from the Maoists of the previous century. The modern insurgents' goals are more limited. They seek to destabilize and dominate an already weak or failed state rather than create an alternative political order. Creating chaos does not require that the militant group have a counter system of government to take the place of the one they destroy. This new, asymmetric, networked approach is aimed not at winning by the conventional defeat of the enemy's armed forces, but rather, by directly influencing the political will of the decision-makers. Such conflicts are almost certain to be lengthy, measured in decades rather than months or years.[14] Dr. Donald Hanle, in his book, *Terrorism: The Newest Face of Warfare* quotes the nineteenth-century Russian terrorist Stepniak-Kravchinsky as saying, "the strong is vanquished, not by the arms of his adversary, but by the continuous tension of his own strength, which exhausts him."[15]

Since they do not seek to replace the existing order in the near term with one of their own, they do not need a strong central leadership. They rely more on a cellular structure with cells "exercising greater autonomy and less connectivity than the old formal networks."[16] Therefore, they have almost no central leadership and compensate for this lack of a rigid, disciplined hierarchy by emphasizing operational and ideological cohesion among the rank and file at all levels.[17] These modern networks are "characterized by non-state actors, linked by pre-existing ties (religion, family, or tribe) that are adapted to support insurgent warfare."

The dense jungles of the classic insurgency have been replaced by the mega-urban centers of today. Distance from the government centers is exchanged for dense urban environments where law enforcement, intelligence, and conventional military assets may not be as effective. Due to the density of this environment, separation of the insurgents from the population is not as feasible a counterinsurgency strategy. These dense, modern industrial societies also provide a target-rich environment for terrorists.[18]

Modern insurgents find that they can be indirectly supported by criminal activities and other external agencies and are not as reliant on the local population for support. Also, due to modern global connectivity, the insurgents' support base may come from a much wider global population. Thanks to a more diverse support base, insurgents may elect to ignore the civilian population or simply intimidate it to remain neutral through acts of terrorism.[19]

The overall strategy of modern insurgencies differ from the classic insurgencies of the 1950's and 1960's that followed Mao's model. Their strategy, as much as a dispersed group can have a macro strategy, is to maintain a barrage of terrorist attacks against government forces and/or their collaborators, whether they are supporters or occupiers. The insurgents' goals are to inflict enough casualties to cause the foreign forces to withdraw and the government to cease to function.[20]

Terrorism Defined

Spurned by ethnic separatist violence following World War I, the League of Nations produced a draft treaty that first defined terrorism in the 1930s. It stated that "all criminal acts directed against a State and intended or calculated to create a state of terror in the minds of particular persons or a group of persons or the general public" was terrorism.[21]

This was not the last time terrorism was defined. A standard definition of terrorism has been hard to pin down. The United States Law Code *U.S. Code Title 22, Ch.38, Para. 2656f(d)*, which guides the US Intelligence Community in defining terrorism, states that terrorism "means premeditated, politically motivated violence perpetrated against noncombatant targets by subnational groups or clandestine agents."[22] The Federal Bureau of Investigation (FBI) defines terrorism as, "the unlawful use of force or violence against persons or property to intimidate or coerce a government, the civilian population, or any segment thereof, in furtherance of political or social objectives."[23] The Council of Arab Ministers of the Interior and the Ministers of Justice defined terrorism at their Arab Convention for the Suppression of Terrorism in Cairo, Egypt, 1998, as

> Any act or threat of violence, whatever its motives or purposes, that occurs in the advancement of an individual or collective criminal agenda and seeking to sow panic among people, causing fear by harming them, or placing their lives, liberty or security in danger, or seeking to cause damage to the environment or to public or private installations or property or to occupying or seizing them, or seeking to jeopardize a national resource.[24]

Although terrorism has been defined by a myriad of groups with a diversity of interests, these definitions all have certain elements that are consistent. Terrorism is intended to create a state of fear in a population. It is intended to create apprehension regarding their chosen course of collective action, whether it is political, social, economic, or military action. The target of terrorism is a state's policymakers. Terrorists intimidate through the threat of violence. They kidnap or murder noncombatant civilians with the intention of changing the policies of that population's government. Democratically elected governments are particularly vulnerable.

State sponsorship of terrorism takes many forms. It usually refers to the state's using terror tactics to subvert and intimidate its own people. The ruling factions of a country will use violence and the threat of violence to discourage activism by its citizens for whatever causes the state deems dangerous to the regime's survival. These methods are most often against what the international community and any civic-minded individual would consider legal or moral and are usually excessively violent. These subversive tactics are meant to terrorize the public into acquiescence with the ruling apparatus's will.

Another form of state sponsorship of terrorism is directed outwardly against people or groups deemed enemies of the state. States have engaged in assassinations and kidnappings of its citizens who are actively engaged in dissident behavior directed against it from the security of another's borders.

This book explores terrorism directed by a state against a population of another country, not its own citizens. The state does not engage in the acts directly, rather through a surrogate carrying out the state's bidding. These activities directed against another nation's population or interests are under official state sanction, although such authorization is rarely acknowledged openly.[25]

State-Sponsored Terrorism

State sponsors of terror regard terrorism as a legitimate tactic toward achieving strategic purposes. Contrary to the statements made by politicians and journalists following horrific terrorist attacks, these attacks are seldom senseless violence. State sponsors employ terrorism "to create certain conditions that, in turn, improve the probability of achieving a given end."[26] They see terrorism as a weapon in the hands of the weak and oppressed against the stronger aggressor. State sponsors of terror use terrorism to influence conflicts that are beyond their national strength because it is a relatively inexpensive force multiplier compared to the conventional strength needed to face a state with resources such as those of the United States.

The sponsor of a surrogate terrorist group (or faction of a legitimate organization that uses terrorism) must maintain links with the fledgling group to send the proper messages to the target. However, the link must be amorphous enough so there can be plausible deniability of the relationship with the perpetrators of the terrorist acts. In order to be effective, the relationship between a state and their surrogate terrorists must remain covert. This method of covert and/or clandestine activity is a common method employed in the conduct of asymmetric or unconventional warfare.

Tactics

The *US Army and Marine Corps Counterinsurgency Field Manual*, states that violent activities of insurgents fall into three categories: conventional, guerrilla, and terrorist.[27] Conventional activity falls outside of the scope of this book. But it is important that the distinction be made between a guerrilla and a terrorist. Both of these terms refer to a tactic employed by insurgents and are not their own category of organized resistance by a group of non-state actors against a state. *Guerrilla* and *terrorist* are not terms that describe strategies or philosophies. They are tools employed by a diverse number of organizations that utilize violence, in this case, insurgents.

The essential features employed by guerrilla fighters are those of "avoiding the enemy's strength, clever use of the terrain, and striking at outposts and logistical support centers from unexpected locations."[28] Terrorists and/or guerrillas may be embedded in and subordinate to insurgency. However, a major difference between the two is that "terrorism may also exist outside of insurgency, animated by sheer revulsion toward the status quo, without offering or striving for an alternative."[29]

The distinction between terrorist and insurgent is blurred. Yassir Arafat of the Palestinian Liberation Organization (PLO) played on this confusion at his address to the United Nations General Assembly in 1974 when he stated, "one man's terrorist is another man's freedom fighter." He went on to say that "the difference between the revolutionary and the terrorist lies in the reason for which each fights."[30] This was clearly an attempt to justify a tactic that intentionally targets non-combatants by equating terrorists with an irregular group more similar to a militia.

Modern insurgents often use terrorism to defeat their opponents through psychological warfare rather that force-on-force military confrontation. The terrorists seek to morally isolate the regime from the mass of the populace and/or large portions of the elite. The government will then find it increasingly difficult to raise taxes. The government will also have difficulty finding willing replacements for its armed forces and police if these instruments of protection for the population are deemed too weak or too inept to stop the violence.[31]

Insurgents may use terrorist tactics to coerce and intimidate a populace, eliminate opponents, publicize their cause, and provoke overreaction on the government's part. They seek to force their target, often the policymakers of their enemy, to react in a certain way. Often the target government will overreact or underreact. Either outcome serves the terrorist's purpose by undermining the government's legitimacy.[32] If the government underreacts, it is breaking its civil contract with its constituents to protect them from harm. If they overreact by utilizing violent and indiscriminate repression and excessive restrictions of citizens' rights, the government risks moving people toward sympathy with the insurgents.

Beware the Dangers of Analytical Shortcomings

This book takes a historical look at how the newly empowered Islamic Theocracy of Iran created its surrogate terrorist organization, Lebanese Hizballah, in the early 1980s to exert influence in the Lebanese Civil War and project power in the greater region. It also shows how from an analytical standpoint one may predict future occurrences of similar events. Therefore, a brief understanding of the potential shortcomings of the human mind with regards to processing information is helpful.

The human mind has difficulty coping with complicated, probabilistic relationships. Our cognitive limitations cause us to employ various simplifying strategies and rules of thumb to ease the burden of mentally processing information to make judgments and decisions. Analysts tend to use these strategies to reduce the burden of processing such information. These strategies can be referred to as mental models. Mental models are critical in allowing individuals to process what otherwise would be an incomprehensible volume of information.

These rules of thumb are useful in helping analysts deal with complexity and ambiguity but can lead to predictably faulty judgments. People have a subconscious mental procedure for processing information. These simplified information-processing strategies can cause mental errors.[33]

All individuals assimilate and evaluate information through the medium of mental models, also referred to as "mindsets." Mindsets can be described as assumptions and expectations that strongly influence what information analysts will accept. Data that are in accordance with analysts' unconscious mental models are more likely to be perceived and remembered than information that is at odds with them. While mindsets are necessary to make sense of large quantities of information, there are risks involved when an analyst succumbs to relying too heavily on mindsets, whether knowingly or not. Analysts tend to perceive what they want to perceive, or what their experiences tell them they should perceive. Once these mindsets or expectations are formed they are resistant to change. New information is assimilated into these existing mental models, sometimes erroneously. If conflicting information that does not fit is discovered, there is a danger that it could be dismissed or ignored.[34]

In intelligence analysis, key information is often lacking. Analysts need to recognize what evidence is lacking and factor this into their calculations. They must estimate the potential impact of the missing data and adjust confidence in their judgment accordingly. Analysts should consider whether the absence of information is normal or is itself an indicator of unusual activity or inactivity.

People often fail to recognize that a particular belief rests on inadequate evidence. Because of this, the belief enjoys an illusion of validity.[35] Reasons why information is often less than perfect are sometimes placed on the shoulders of the analyst. Their misunderstanding, misperception, and lack of a complete understanding of the situation can lead to faulty advice. But the analyst is not always at fault. Bias on the part of the source of the information or a distortion in the reporting chain from subsource to the person collecting the information to analyst can lead to the same skewed intelligence product.[36]

Analysts tend to use different criteria to evaluate conclusions they desire. For conclusions they want to believe, they ask only that the evidence not force them to believe otherwise.[37]

For conclusions they choose not to believe, contrary evidence is often carefully scrutinized and transformed into evidence that is considered relatively uninformative, assigned little weight, considered too flawed to be relevant, or redefined into a less damaging category.[38]

In processing information of uncertain accuracy or reliability, analysts tend to make a simple yes or no decision. If they reject the evidence, they tend to reject it fully so it plays no further role in their mental calculations. If they accept the evidence, they tend to accept it wholly at face value ignoring the probabilistic nature of the accuracy or reliability judgment.[39]

When a person believes that the existence of one event implies the existence of the other, this is described as correlation. In relation to the study at hand, this can be particularly dangerous. Inaccurate perception of correlation leads to inaccurate perception of cause and effect. Illusory correlation occurs when people perceive a relationship that does not in fact exist.[40] This can be especially dangerous when an analyst is comparing a model to actual events on the ground.

There are many other pitfalls related to how analysts perceive and accept new information. People often focus on instances that support the existence of a relationship but ignore those cases that fail to support it. They also remember occurrences more readily than non-occurrences. People judge the probability of an event by the ease with which they can imagine relevant instances of similar events or the number of such events that they can easily remember. Events that are likely to occur are easier to imagine than unlikely events. For instance, if no reasonable scenario comes to mind, then the event is deemed impossible or highly unlikely. If several scenarios come easily to mind, or if one scenario is particularly compelling, then the event in question appears probable. The ability to recall instances of an event is influenced by how recently the event occurred, whether the analysts were personally involved, whether there are vivid and memorable details, and how important it seemed to them at the time.

Analysts may filter out pertinent information if it does not fit into the list of predetermined indicators. This is a danger when comparing information to a model an analyst is expecting an adversary to follow and not taking into account that events in the real world are fluid. This indicator list could be incomplete due to changes in enemy modus operandi, changes in intelligence collection capabilities, or analysts neglecting evidence when they create the indicator list.

Another common occurrence in information analysis is "mirror-imaging." Mirror-imaging involves analysts' filling gaps in their own knowledge by assuming that the other side is likely to act in a certain way because that is how they themselves would act. They similarly risk failure of analysis when they assume their adversary's leaders think like their leaders do. Judgment must be based on how the other leaders perceive what is in their best interest. When they think their beliefs or actions are the result of external elements, they assume that those elements would have a similar influence on others. Thus, they infer that other people would tend to think or act likewise.[41]

A common misperception is that people in other cultures think the way we do. In general, people are less aware that the same issue or situation is construed quite differently by different people.[42] Trying to think like them often results in applying the logic of one's own culture and experience to try to understand the actions of others, without knowing that one is using the logic of one's own culture.[43] Cultural differences may weigh heavily on a foreign leader's decision-making process. The Sapir-Whorf hypothesis explains that language and thought are inseparable; therefore, different languages mean different ways of thinking.[44]

In addition to analysts, policy makers are also subject to information-processing errors. Members of highly cohesive advisory groups who are under considerable pressure to devise effective courses of action can become overly concerned with maintaining apparent consensus within the group and will sometimes censor their personal reservations to accomplish it. This phenomenon is called "groupthink." Because so much disagreement remains hidden, beliefs are not properly shaped by healthy debate and scrutiny. This may lead individuals to exaggerate the extent to which other people believe the same way they do.[45]

Understanding Denial and Deception

To establish a common understanding of what denial and deception (D&D) are as they pertain to this book, a brief discussion of these processes follows. Denial and deception can be instruments used to shape the environment so that a state or non-state actor can better achieve its strategic objectives. The objective of D&D is to get the target of the operation to react in a way that better suits the practitioner's interests. Denial and Deception seeks to engender errors in the perceptual apparatus of the target with the goal of causing bad decisions.[46] It is a force multiplier mainly used by the weak against the strong, and can be used in times of peace and of war. Most information collected by an intelligence service is not part of a D&D effort. This is to say that most D&D efforts use elements of truth to establish credibility.

Denial can be defined as attempts made to block channels by which an adversary or target could find truth, thus preventing them from acting in a timely manner. Denial efforts seek to impair, impede, degrade, or otherwise prevent intelligence collection. Roy Godson and James J. Wirtz define denial as "the actions and programs that foreign countries (or other intelligence targets) undertake to prevent us from succeeding in our most basic mission, namely the collection of secret information by secret means."[47] It is easier for an adversary to deny than deceive.

Deception seeks to mask, misdirect, or confuse the target of the deception. It is an effort to cause the enemy to believe something that is not true. The purpose of incorporating deception planning into a larger strategic operation is to persuade the enemy that you are somewhere else; your weapons and forces are different from what they are; you intend to do something else, somewhere else, at a different time, and in a different manner; your knowledge of the enemy is either greater or less than it really is; or his operations are either more or less successful than they actually are.

The most difficult and crucial part of detecting and exposing a denial and deception operation being directed at you is acknowledging that you are vulnerable to it. You must have a thorough understanding of the D&D process and what steps the deceiver needs to take to successfully execute a deception operation if you wish to detect a D&D operation's being directed against you.

When conducting such an operation, the enemy must consider myriad variables and be prepared for unintended consequences. The deceiver must use unwitting people in order to maintain the utmost secrecy. Every deception has flaws; the analyst just has to be looking for them. The greatest chance of making a mistake is in the implementation phase of the operation, not in the planning phase.

Analysts must put themselves in the position of the enemy not only by imagining what they would do in the enemy's position, but also analyzing what the enemy would do in this circumstance. When trying to expose a D&D operation being directed against them, analysts should look for intelligence gaps and anomalies. When determining what indicators are important to this particular situation, they should acknowledge that the absence of evidence does not necessarily mean that evidence does not exist. Just because there is no evidence of a certain situation, does not mean that it did not happen. The very purpose of denial is to mask part of the operation.

According to Godson and Wirtz, "seen from the perspective of the intelligence customer, our truth-telling ability in intelligence is jeopardized by successful denial and deception conducted by foreign countries about whom we seek truthful information."[48] They go on to explain that, "the future effectiveness of US intelligence depends inordinately on our ability to understand and to counter foreign D&D."[49]

This book shows how Iran has used and continues to use terrorist surrogates to counter US presence in the Persian Gulf region. The objective of Iran's foreign D&D campaign is to enhance, devalue, or change the truth communicated by a state or non-state actor that wants to affect a target policymaker's decisions.

Notes

1. Anthony J. Schwarz, "Iraq's Militias: The True Threat to Coalition Success," *Parameters*, XXXVII (Spring 2007): 57-58.

2. Schwarz, *Parameters*, 61.

3. Schwarz, *Parameters*, 56-58.

4. Schwarz, *Parameters*, 59.

5. Frank G. Hoffman, "Neo-Classical Counterinsurgency?" *Parameters*, XXXVII (Summer 2007): 81.

6. Daniel S. Roper, "Global Counterinsurgency: Strategic Clarity for the Long War," *Parameters*, XXXVIII (Autumn 2008): 95-96.

7. Roper, *Parameters*, 94.

8. Hoffman, *Parameters*, 71.

9. Donald J. Hanle, *Terrorism: The Newest Face of Warfare* (New York: Pergamon-Brassey's International Defense Publishing, Inc., 1989), 133.

10. Hanle, 134-136.

11. Martin J. Muckian, "Structural Vulnerabilities of Networked Insurgencies: Adapting to the New Adversary," *Parameters*, XXXVI (Winter 2006): 17.

12. Hoffman, *Parameters*, 76.

13. Muckian, *Parameters*, 15-16.

14. Brian Reed, "A Social Network Approach to Understanding an Insurgency," *Parameters*, XXXVII (Summer 2007): 24.

15. Hanle, 144.

16. Hoffman, *Parameters*, 75.

17. Muckian, *Parameters*, 16.

18. Hanle, 143.

19. Hoffman, *Parameters*, 76-81.

20. Muckian, *Parameters*, 16-18.

21. Jane Boulden, Thomas George Weiss, *Terrorism and the UN: before and after September 11* (Indiana University Press, 2004), 178.

22. *Cornell University Law School*, "Legal Information Institute", URL: < http://www.law.cornell.edu/uscode/22/usc_sec_22_00002656—f000-.html >, accessed 5 June 2009.

23. *FBI Baltimore Office*, "Domestic Terrorism Program", URL: <http:// baltimore.fbi.gov/domter.htm>, accessed 5 June 2009.

24. *www.al-bab.com*, "Arab Convention on Terrorism", URL: <http:// www.al-bab.com/arab/docs/league/terrorism98.htm>, accessed 5 June 2009.

25. *Terrorism Research*, "State Sponsored Terrorism", URL: <http:// www.terrorism-research.com/state/>, accessed 5 June 2009.

26. Hanle, 108.

27. *The U.S. Army/Marine Corps Counterinsurgency Field Manual* (Chicago: The University of Chicago Press, 2007) 108.

28. Reed, *Parameters*, 22.

29. Roper, *Parameters*, 94.

30. Roper, *Parameters*, 95.

31. Hanle, 142.

32. Roper, *Parameters*, 96-97.

33. Richards J. Heuer, Jr., *Psychology of Intelligence Analysis* (Washington DC: Center for the Study of Intelligence, Central Intelligence Agency, 1999) 111.

34. Heuer, 9-14.

35. Thomas Gilovich, *How We Know What Isn't So; The Fallibility of Human Reason in Everyday Life* (New York: The Free Press, 1991) 30.

36. Heuer, 122.

37. Gilovich, 83.

38. Gilovich, 55-56.

39. Heuer, 122.

40. Heuer, 140-141.

41. Heuer, 69-71.

42. Gilovich, 115-117.

43. Dr. Rob Johnston, *Analytic Culture in the U.S. Intelligence Community; An Ethnographic Study* (Washington DC: Center for the Study of Intelligence, Central Intelligence Agency, 2005) 76.

44. Johnston, 17.

45. Gilovich, 122.

46. Scott Gerwehr and Russell W. Glenn, *Unweaving the Web; Deception and Adaptation in Future Urban Operations* (Rand Arroyo Center, 2002) 44.

47. Roy Godson and James J. Wirtz, *Strategic Denial and Deception* (New Brunswick, USA: Transaction Publications, 2002) 230.

48. Godson and Wirtz, 229.

49. Godson and Wirtz, 230.

Acknowledgments

This book is dedicated to the men and women who serve in our armed forces, intelligence community, and law enforcement.

When the decisions are made by our policymakers to engage an adversary or enemy, they respond, right or wrong, like it or not, to protect America and to serve her best interests. Some of them endure hardships in dangerous places far from home. Some must face our country's enemies in our own neighborhoods. But all forego the semblance of a normal life as they face down those who wish to murder our fellow Americans in the name of whatever they may label their cause. They miss birthdays, anniversaries, and first words. They work long days, nights, weekends, and holidays under insufferable circumstances so that their families and friends can enjoy the security and amenities that they sometimes take for granted. So, on behalf of all of us who wish to show our appreciation of the job you do and the life you and your families endure, I dedicate this book to you.

I would like to acknowledge the following colleagues for their help in editing the content of this book: Adam P., Greg K., Greg T., Steve McB., Heather L., "Murphy", and my brother for his help with my grammar.

I would especially like to express my deepest gratitude for their support and encouragement to my wife, my family, and JB . . . *SUPER, GREAT, AND GETTING BETTER!*

Introduction

Today, National Security is embroiled in the unknown, the uncertain, the unseen, and the unexpected. State security has become more dependent on international security and stability, not just its own and that of its neighbors. Space and time have become compressed. Distant actions have local effects, and local actions can have global effects. States can no longer hide behind walls, borders or oceans. These physical borders have been breached by globalization and information technology.[1]

In the twenty-first century, information technology and globalization, failed states, rogue states, ethnic militias and radical extremists produce substate transnational actors involved in conflicts. Power has been redistributed among states, markets, and civil structures. There is a greater reliance on interdependence and interconnectivity.[2]

Iran's use of Lebanese Hizballah as a surrogate organization—an aspect of its power projection regionally during the 1980s—was an excellent example of the transition from the traditional state-centered paradigm ordered around conventional strength between rival states to a new type of warfare practiced today. Research on Iranian activities in the region, especially that of the Ministry of Intelligence and Security (MOIS) and the Iranian Revolutionary Guard Corps-Quds Force (IRGC-QF), since the Islamic Revolution of 1979, served as a basis for developing a model that must be followed in order to create a successful state sponsored surrogate organization. Lebanese Hizballah is a complex organization that uses a wide spectrum of tactics and programs to achieve its goals. These include militant resistance, social services, political activism, and terrorism. By studying how a successful surrogate organization like Lebanese Hizballah was formed by Iran, one can better understand what the necessary conditions are to create and maintain such an organization. This book will also explain what elements were essential to the success of Lebanese Hizballah and how Iran was able to support this.

If one understands the factors required to create a state-sponsored surrogate organization that uses terrorism as one of its tools to achieve its goals, one can better predict the conditions necessary, the actions that the state sponsor needs to take, and the types of individuals it needs. By studying a model of what has worked, analysts can establish a list of indicators and warning signals to confirm their suspicions that a state-sponsored surrogate is being directed against them. They can then better understand what they are not—but should—be seeing.

When studying Iran's creation and effective use of Lebanese Hizballah, a model of conditions and activities emerges. Thus from a state's perspective, a surrogate group can be created when four elements are present.

1. existence of an area under conflict
2. creation of the surrogate group
3. creation of ambiguities to avoid responsibility/blame
4. maintenance

Additionally, the study of Iran indicates another "characteristic" of the state sponsor that must be present: tolerance. A surrogate often acts out of self-interest, which may not always coincide with the interests of the state sponsor. This book also explores the dynamics of the relationship between the state sponsor and the surrogate organization over time. As the organization matures and grows in strength, they will become more independent and less willing to be directed or controlled by the state sponsor. The group will also develop other sources to supply them with money, equipment, and weapons, to some degree taxing the patience and tolerance of the state sponsor for continuing support and assistance.

The basis for this model's conditions, activities and characteristics emerges from the following analysis of Iran's struggle to reach its strategic national goals for the Persian Gulf Region.

Iran's Strategic Goals

Since the inception of the Islamic Republic in 1979, Iran's national strategic goals have been to increase their influence in the Persian Gulf Region and decrease the US presence there. They have sought to expand their economic and cultural ties with their neighbors (except Israel), enlarge their sphere of influence, and resist US military and political presence and policies.[3] Iran has systematically attempted to influence the outcome of regional conflicts in support of its national strategic goals. The successful employment of groups such as Lebanese Hizballah has allowed Iran to increase its regional influence while countering US diplomatic, economic, and conventional military strength.

The Islamic Republic has taken on an expansive philosophy. They are ambitious for status and believe they deserve to be consulted on any issue of regional importance. Iran seeks to gain leverage in the Middle East peace process, intimidate or subvert countries within its sphere of influence into changing policies, and change the policies of or eject foreign foes in the Middle East, all while avoiding direct involvement.[4]

The Iranian leadership sees Iran leading the Islamic world in resisting the US military and American cultural influence within the Persian Gulf region.[5] Most Iranians perceive their nation as a great civilization that has been deprived of its "rightful" status as a regional superpower by foreign intervention, mainly from the US and Great Britain.[6] Iran sees the US presence in the area today as a regional destabilizing factor and a threat to its national security.[7] Due to the immense military and economic might of the United States, terrorism through surrogates has been an attractive option for Tehran. It is clandestine, coercive, and non-attributable. "It provides the state the means to avoid the two extremes of, on the one hand, direct involvement (which might entail confrontation) and, on the other, total abstention (with a dimunition [sic] in influence)."[8]

Iran's regional influence is being challenged in many areas. It may be feeling pressure from the United States which has conducted very successful military campaigns in the countries on Iran's eastern and western borders. Iran may feel that the "Great Satan" is closing in on them, as a possible next target. The United States will gain an economic advantage in the region as well as a military advantage when the insurgencies in Iraq and Afghanistan are quieted.

The liberation of Afghanistan could see the opening of an oil and gas pipeline from Central Asia through a friendly Afghanistan and Pakistan. Iranian oil may be hurt further by major oil company investment in a free Iraq at the expense of Iran.[9]

The clerics in Iran also may feel threatened by the liberation of Najaf and Karbala in Iraq, two of the holiest cities in Shia Islam, since the Iranians have enjoyed rule from their holy city of Qom. Najaf hosts about 20,000 Iranian pilgrims per month who visit the Imam Ali Shrine there. The city is reviving with improved security and less political repression and might eventually meet pre-war expectations that it would again exceed Iran's Qom as the heart of the Shiite theological world.[10]

Iran's goal when it formed Lebanese Hizballah in 1982 was to drive the Israelis and Western powers out of Lebanon. This was accomplished when the Iranians expelled US and multinational peacekeeping forces from Beirut in 1983 by employing terrorist tactics that could not be directly attributed to Iran. In May 2000, Iran achieved another success when, after eighteen years of guerrilla conflict and terrorist activity, Israel left Southern Lebanon. This action on the part of Israel seemed to reinforce Iran's broader goal to drive the West out of the Middle East, or at least force a change in the West's policies in the region.

Iran's Strategy

Iran realizes that, at least in the near term, it does not have to drive the United States out of the Middle East completely; but only to perpetuate an unstable environment. It is important for Iran to maintain deniability so as not to draw the United States into a full-scale military conflict.

Iran's strategy to achieve their national goal is to use asymmetric warfare in the form of surrogate terrorist organizations to counter US presence in the region. This strategy and the methods used have changed little since the beginning of rule by the Islamic clerics in 1979. Basically, Iran relies on asymmetric warfare carried out by its Special Forces and Intelligence Service. These organizations employ denial and deception through the use of surrogate terrorist groups to undermine US strengths and objectives for the region. This method has a low cost with a high yield. Creating and funding terrorist organizations is much more cost effective than trying to compete with the United States in a conventional military competition. Iran sees terrorism as an instrument of state policy for strategic purposes. Thus, terrorism is an instrument of coercion and intimidation that Iran has unleashed and will continue to use on the United States as well as on its own neighbors.

The use of surrogate terrorists groups has proven successful for Iran in the past. Iran influenced the outcome of the Lebanese Civil War through its creation and use of the terrorist organization, Hizballah, or the "Party of God." Iran has also aided the Palestinian terrorist groups Islamic Jihad and HAMAS in their fight for land against Israel.

Use of Asymmetric Warfare by Special Forces and Intelligence Services

There are two organizations in the Iranian intelligence and defense sectors that help Tehran achieve its national goals through the use of surrogate terrorist groups. These groups are the Iranian Revolutionary Guards Corps (IRGC) including the Quds Force, their special operations forces, and the Ministry of Intelligence and Security (MOIS). At times these groups' spheres of influence have been seen to overlap in the execution of Iran's strategy. However, each has been and will continue to be a dominant player in Iran's quest for influence in the region.

The IRGC, mostly by tradition and/or law, is not accountable to parliament, but only to the Supreme Leader.[11] They were initially set up in 1979 as the internal security apparatus to consolidate Ayatollah Khomeini's grip on the Iranian population. The IRGC grew to be the primary tool for promoting Khomeini's doctrines. Their agents occupy positions at Iranian embassies across Europe, Africa, and Asia under diplomatic cover.[12] The Quds (Jerusalem) Force is the most elite of the five units of the IRGC. It is made up of about 1,000 hand-picked men who receive training in all aspects of terrorism, assassination, and guerrilla fighting. They have trained scores of foreign terrorist groups. During the early 1990s the Quds Force was responsible for the assassinations of anti-Khomeini exiles.[13]

The MOIS is the principle civilian intelligence and security organization in Iran. The MOIS was formed in 1984 and is the direct descendant of the SAVAK (National Intelligence and Security Organization), the Shah's brutal intelligence and security organization. It is headquartered in the Pasdaran section of Tehran. The MOIS is subordinate to the Office of the President but has a close, less formal relationship with the Supreme Leader.

Use of D&D in the Form of a Surrogate Terrorist Organization

Terrorism is defined by Amal Saad-Ghorayeb, an Assistant Professor at the Lebanese American University, as "any premeditated act of violence against innocent civilians that seeks to create an atmosphere of fear in order to influence a specific audience."[14] She further explains that it is a deliberate attempt to terrorize a civilian population for political ends. Dr. Donald J. Hanle, a professor at the Joint Military Intelligence College in Washington D.C., defines terrorism as a form of warfare.

> Terrorism meets the same basic criteria as war. It represents consciously selected force applied for a specific end . . . terrorism represents a clash of wills between two contending parties. If both parties employ force to resolve a clash of wills, and if both parties seek a political end through this conflict, then a state of war exists, and the terrorism used by either belligerent constitutes a form of war.[15]

Iran sees terrorism as an instrument of state policy for strategic purposes. By employing terrorism, Iran can advance its national goal of expanding regional influence with resources that do not match its ambitions.

One example that demonstrates that approach is Lebanese Hizballah. As a surrogate, Lebanese Hizballah allowed Tehran to engage in regional conflicts while denying involvement. In addition, Lebanese Hizballah has enabled Iran to avoid force on force conflict with its enemies that are militarily superior. Thus, by keeping Lebanese Hizballah trained, supported and engaged with its enemies, Iran has been able to further its national goals in the region.

How Iran's Strategy Has Changed Since the Islamic Revolution

Ayatollah Ruhollah Khomenei built the central government of Iran after the 1979 Islamic Revolution around the concepts of independence, freedom, and Velayat-e Faqih, or the infallibility of a Supreme Leader. His core belief was that since sovereignty lies with God, opposition is blasphemy.[16] Khomenei wanted Iran to play a leading role in international affairs. However, his ambitions outweighed Iran's resources. Thus, he recognized early on that an asymmetric strategy using terrorist surrogate groups would have to be used to give Iran leverage in regional events.

By the time Ayatollah Khomeini died in 1989, Iran had found itself isolated globally and friendless in the region as a result of ten years of using terrorism to intimidate and subvert its neighbors and any other country that opposed Iran's policies. Iran had confirmed its status as a pariah state.[17]

In June 1989 following the death of Ayatollah Khomeini, the Assembly of Experts, the body charged with electing the Supreme Leader, elected Ayatollah al-Udhma Sayyid Ali Khamenei the Supreme Leader of the Islamic Republic. The Assembly is made up of eighty-six senior Islamic clerics that are elected every eight years.[18] As Supreme Leader he was appointed for life. Overall, Khamenei is an idealist. He believes in the justness of the Islamic theocracy that Khomenei created. Khamenei sees Iran leading the world of Islam in resisting the US military and cultural interference in the Persian Gulf region.[19] He also sees Iran as the model for revolutionary Islam.

Khamenei, the Supreme Leader, along with the Council of Guardians (COG), all of whom are conservative, hard-line Islamic clerics, dominate the activities of the central government. They can bar candidates from running for elections and reject legislation passed by the Majlis—the national Parliament—that does not conform to Islamic law.[20] It is the constitutional duty of the Majlis to scrutinize the government's budget and economic policy.[21]

The same year that Khomeini died, Ali Akbar Hashemi Rafsanjani was inaugurated as President. He would serve two terms during the period after the 1980-88 Iran-Iraq War that he termed the "era of reconstruction." His terms were plagued by rampant materialism throughout the country as Iran suddenly returned to the international marketplace. There was a growing disparity in wealth as informal networks of cartels of business associates, unregulated and avaricious, were established.[22] Rafsanjani was very unpopular but was acknowledged as a master political operator. Later in his political career, he would go on to chair the powerful and hard-liner dominated Assembly of Experts and the Expediency Council.[23]

By 1997, 65% of the population of Iran was under thirty years of age. The young population was disenchanted with the rule of the clerics and saw them as mismanaging the country's vast economic resources. The clerics also saw that their policies on terrorism had been somewhat counterproductive. Iran was friendless in the region and beyond. Public opinion had shifted against the lone wolf, militant approach to regional and world politics. The hardliners accepted that they needed to make some accommodations to this generation.

The hardliners were willing to accommodate the young populace by standing by and allowing a reformist to be elected President. In 1997, Mohammad Hojjatoleslam Khatami was elected President of Iran and would serve two terms. The President is elected by the public to no more than two, four-year terms and the Supreme Leader must confirm the people's choice. Khatami ran on a platform that called for normalization of Iran's relationship with its neighbors in the Gulf and with European Union countries. He was more of a realist than the Supreme Leader, Khamenei. Khatami saw Iran as a model for Islamic democracy rather than Islamic theocracy. He felt that Iran's greatest contribution to the region was improving on this Islamic democratic model rather than intervening in the business of other countries.[24] When Khatami was elected to the Presidency, he wanted to assure Iran's neighbors that Iran had given up its attempts at subversion. Also, by allowing Khatami to run for and win the Presidency, the clerics were able to give world leaders someone to at least attempt normal relations with.

Khatami sought to support the suffering Iranian economy with proper foreign investment.[25] He believed the fiscal policy was in need of fundamental reform. He hoped to support this policy by moving away from a closed economy and opening Iran up to foreign investment. However, after eight years as President, the popular President was largely ineffectual in his efforts to open the economy.[26] His terms were plagued by a lack of progress, whether due to his policies or from interference from the more conservative and powerful clerics.[27]

Given the internal and external front put forth by the powerful hard-liners, they realized that they also needed to curb terrorist meddling in the region. Terrorism with autonomy had become more difficult and the conservative hard-liners saw that they needed to allow some flexibility in Iran's foreign policies related to their current use of terrorism.

In the mid-to-late 1990s, however, several events kept Iran's support of terrorism in the spotlight. In 1996, Iran was blamed for the terrorist attack on the Khobar Towers in Saudi Arabia, used to house US Air Force personnel, in which nineteen people were killed. Iran came dangerously close to being attacked by the United States in retribution. However, due to the ambiguity of the situation, neither the United States nor Israel pursued a military response. Saudi Arabia, a US ally in the region, was afraid of Iranian retaliation if the United States struck. Iran also voiced its willingness to raise the cost of a conflict by threatening regional instability.[28]

Also, in April 1997, the German courts named Iranian officials directly responsible for the killings of Iranian Kurds in Berlin. Thus far Iran had never had to pay the price of a military response by the United

States or any other country for its support of terrorism, though the world was losing its patience.[29]

In 2005, Khatami completed his second term as President. In the years prior to Khatami's departure from office, Khamenei had succeeded in seating a docile Majlis to open the way for unification of a fractured political system. Khamenei and the hard-liners in the Council of Guardians accomplished this by barring nearly 4,000 candidates from running in the January 2004 Parliamentary elections including 80 current members.[30] This resulted in a landslide for the conservatives who favored Khamenei and thus the clerics dominated the new Parliament. Prior to this, Khatami and the reformers held a commanding majority in the Majlis.

With their new command of the Majlis and continued domination of other institutions of power, the conservatives sought to reform the political landscape in their favor. They sought to do this through political and economic populism, repression of civil liberties, and by sustaining a continuing crisis in foreign relations to keep attention focused abroad.[31] In the presidential elections of 2005, the former mayor of Tehran, Mahmoud Ahmadinejad, would play only one part of this broad, hard-line conservative attempt to seize power.[32]

Ahmadinejad is the antithesis of Khatami. He is ultra-conservative in his political views and eccentric in his religious beliefs. His stated goals of his presidency have been to establish the hegemony of hard-line conservatism and to restore the Islamic revolution to its true path. Ahmadinejad claimed "[T]he revolution had lost its way under the presidency of Rafsanjani and the pollution of revolutionary values through the introduction of rampant materialism and the corruption which accompanies it."[33]

In step with the hard-liners' formula for dominating the political landscape in Iran, Ahmadinejad believes the crisis of foreign relations is a constant reality. He agrees with the Iranian sense of victimhood and the national myth that they have been treated in a singularly unjust way at the hands of a treacherous and uncomprehending world.[34] He thinks that knuckling down to a long and thankless fight is Iran's heroic destiny in this hostile world.[35]

Notes

1. Michael Evans, "From Kandesh to Kandahar: Military Theory and the Future of War," *Naval War College Review*, LVI, 3 (Summer 2003).
2. Evans.
3. Gawdat Bahgat, "United States-Iranian Relations: The Terrorism Challenge," *Parameters*, XXXVIII, 4 (Winter 2008-09), 7.
4. Shahram Chubin, *Whither Iran? Reform, Domestic Politics and National Security* (London: Oxford University Press, 2002) 88-89.
5. Chubin, 24.
6. Bahgat, *Parameters*, 9.
7. Chubin, 30.
8. Chubin, 89.
9. *Foreign Affairs*, "Iran in the Balance," URL: < www.foreignaffairs.org/20010701faesay4994/puneet-talwar/iran-in-the-balance.html >, accessed 25 March 2004.
10. Kenneth Katzman, "Iran's Activities and Influence in Iraq," *Congressional Research Service Report for Congress* (Library of Congress, Order Code RS22323, 17 September 2008) 6.
11. Ali M. Ansari, *Iran Under Ahmadinejad: The Politics of Confrontation* (The International Institute for Strategic Studies, Adelphi Paper 393, London: Routledge, 2007) 81.
12. Hala Jaber, *Hezbollah; Born With a Vengeance* (New York: Columbia University Press, 1997) 109-111.
13. Tom Diaz and Barbara Newman, *Lightning Out of Lebanon; Hezbollah Terrorists on American Soil* (New York: Ballantine Books, 2005) 63.
14. Amal Saad-Ghorayeb, *Hizbu'llah: Politics and Religion* (London: Pluto Press, 2002) 146.
15. Donald J. Hanle, *Terrorism: The Newest Face of Warfare* (New York: Pergamon-Brassey's International Defense Publishing, Inc., 1989), 133.
16. *The Economist*, "The Surreal World of Iranian Politics," URL: < http://economist.com.PrinterFriendly.cfm?Story_ID=1522038 >, accessed 17 March 2004.
17. Chubin, 87.
18. Ansari, 86.
19. Chubin, 24.
20. Ansari, 31.
21. Ansari, 84.
22. Ansari, 13-14.
23. Ansari, 87-89.
24. Chubin, 26.
25. Ansari, 17.
26. Ansari, 87.

27. Ansari, 25.

28. Chubin, 49-50.

29. Chubin, 95.

30. *The Economist*, "A Sorry Election," URL: < http://economist.com. PrinterFriendly.cfm?Story_ID=245871 > accessed 17 March 2004.

31. Ansari, 42.

32. Ansari, 32.

33. Ansari, 69.

34. Ansari, 25-26.

35. Ansari, 46.

Disclaimer

All statements of fact, opinion, or analysis expressed are those of the author and do not reflect the official positions or views of any US Government agency. Nothing in the contents should be construed as asserting or implying US Government authentication of information or endorsement of the author's views. This material has been reviewed by the US Government to prevent the disclosure of classified information.

Chapter 1

Existence of an Area Under Conflict

The country or area the state sponsor of terrorism wishes to exert its influence on must be engaged in some sort of conflict. The conflict can be in the form of a civil war or an occupation by a foreign power, or both. "For an insurgency to take root, extraordinary circumstances must exist for the government to lose its authority over some or all of its sovereign territory. Either the state is collapsing or has already collapsed." In either state, the "government is in such a disarray that it lacks the capability to respond to challenges to its authority."[1] Given this condition, the state seeking to exert its influence must choose sides if it is not naturally, through demographics, ideology, religion or ethnicity, drawn to one or another.

Civil War or Foreign Intervention

Lebanon was an ideal place for Iran to create and employ a surrogate group during the Civil War from 1975 to 1990. The situation in Lebanon was chaotic and violent. The fourteen-year civil war was characterized by a confusing mix of militias and government forces from several countries fighting each other in often contradicting alliances. The war often pitted Maronite militias, the Lebanese Army, and the Christian Maronite Phalangists against the Lebanese National Movement, the Palestinians, as well as Druze, Sunni, and Shia Muslims.

The Druze, an offshoot of the Ismaili sect of Shia Islam,[2] dominated the cities of Lebanon and the lowlands. They were based in the south Lebanon Mountains with their stronghold in the Shouf Mountains. The

Maronites, a Christian sect, dominated life in the north Lebanese Mountains. The Maronites and Muslims had been fighting since the fifth century. After World War I, the French received a mandate from the League of Nations, in April 1920, over the regions of modern Syria and Lebanon. When forced to choose between favoring the Muslims or Maronites, they chose the Maronites. This began the Christian domination of Lebanon. The Shia played virtually no part in the early days of this new mandate as they eked out their living in agricultural areas.[3]

The Civil War in Lebanon was a result of feuding among a number of religious and ethnic groups supported by different countries.[4] Between the founding of the state of Israel in 1948 and the Six Day War in 1967, the Palestinian population in Lebanon grew to 350,000.[5] The Muslim population grew much faster in the years following than did the indigenous Christian population. Prior to 1975, Lebanon was very Western; made up of Christians and many different Islamic sects. The majority of the Christians were Maronites.

Christians and Sunni Muslims dominated the economic and political systems, while Shia Muslims constituted roughly 35% of the total Lebanese population.[6] This imbalance frustrated the underrepresented and deprived Shia Muslims and further alienated them. The Shia community suffered from deprivation of resources as well as access to power.[7] They were a distinct religious minority, predominantly rural, poor, disorganized, and lacking an effective clerical leadership.[8]

The fundamentally oppressive Lebanese state was founded on the Maronite community's political supremacy.[9] But this status quo began to be challenged in the 1970s and 1980s. Shia political organizations and militias began to spring up to vie with Christian, Israeli, and Palestinian forces. The Maronite Christians still dominated the government, but now the various Muslim sects constituted a majority of the population in Lebanon.

In September of 1970, the Hashemite King of Jordan, Hussein, tired of the fighting between Israel and the Palestinian Liberation Organization (PLO) based in his country and fearing the potential escalation of the conflict, forced the PLO out. They were pushed into Lebanon; which was too weak to keep them away. Due to this eviction and to the large number of Palestinian refugees in Southern Lebanon resulting from the 1948, 1967, and 1973 wars with Israel, as well as Lebanon's shared border with Israel, the PLO, led by Yassir Arafat, located its bases in southern Lebanon. The Palestinians took over much Shia land in the south, forcing tens of thousands into the cities and into the grips of the civil war.[10]

When the Shia began fleeing the war-zone, many settled in the only areas available to them in the southern suburbs of Beirut. They began building makeshift homes in the vicinity of the city's dump and common sewer. During this time of conflict and population displacement, their political status didn't change. While the Lebanese government felt threatened by the influx of poor Shia into Beirut, they did little to improve their plight. The Sunnis resented them, as this area had historically been their domain. Christian and Druze leaders continued to use their influence to concentrate on improving their own areas.[11]

Two years before their eviction from Jordan, PLO units in southern Lebanon began shelling northern Israel and conducting cross-border raids. The Lebanese Muslims loosely supported the PLO at the time. The Christians were teamed up with the local Phalangist party, a Christian Maronite sect founded by Pierre Gemayel in 1936. The Christians were favored by the Israelis, who saw Lebanon as a Christian country threatened by Muslims. The Christians were afraid that the presence of the Palestinians would disrupt the balance of power and provoke an Israeli invasion. The Druze leader, Kamal Jumblatt, wanted the PLO commandos to have freedom of movement in southern Lebanon to continue their operations.[12] A political rift began to form between the supporters and critics of the PLO's presence in Lebanon, particularly between Shia Muslims and Maronite Christians as a result of Israeli reprisals and Lebanese casualties.

By 1975, Christian, Druze, and Muslim militias had sprung up across Lebanon. Beirut had been split by factions fighting along the Green Line; the no-man's land that separated the Christian east from the Muslim west.[13] A year into the Civil War, Syria came to the aid of the Maronite Christians, who were being pounded by Shia Muslim groups like AMAL.[14] Thus began a much-fractured struggle within Lebanon.

The Shia were largely marginalized in Lebanon until Imam Sayyed Musa as-Sadr emerged in the early 1970s. Sadr was born in Qom, Iran and earned a law degree in Tehran. His father was a distinguished academic scholar who founded a religious university in Qom.[15] After Musa as-Sadr's law studies, he pursued religious studies in Najaf, Iraq, where many of the leading Shia Islamic leading ayatollahs and scholars were based. He organized the Shia of Lebanon and gave them a greater say in the events unfolding. Sadr formed the Movement of the Dispossessed to provide a platform and vehicle to mobilize the Lebanese Shia and pres-

sure the government for socioeconomic reforms.[16] Along with this movement he formed the Shia militia, AMAL, in 1975 to protect Shia rights
and to give this deprived portion of the Lebanese population a more
equitable stake in the conflict.[17] This acronym (*AMAL*) from the words
naming the Lebanese Resistance Detachments is the same as the Arabic
word for *hope*.[18]

Many events helped coalesce this disparate group into a formidable
force. AMAL grew powerful in the early days of the Civil War. When
the War began, the Lebanese Shia in the south were caught in the crossfire
between the entrenched PLO forces and Israeli commandos. This need
for protection united the Shia behind a fast forming organized movement
that not only sought to give the Shia a voice but also arms to back it up.
In 1978, the young movement's founder and leader mysteriously disap-
peared. On 31 August, while on a trip to Libya to see Libyan leader
Muammar Qaddafi, as-Sadr vanished. Also in that year, the Israelis
launched Operation Litani into Lebanon to force the PLO from their
entrenched positions along their common border. An alliance ensued
between Israel and a militia formed by Saad Haddad. His militia, the
South Lebanese Army (SLA), was a proxy of Israel manned mainly by
Christians.[19]

The following year, Ayatollah Khomeini returned to Iran energizing
Shia Muslims everywhere. Khomeini provided strong spiritual and political leadership to Lebanese Shia in the absence of their inspiring leader,
Musa as-Sadr. On 6 June 1982, the Israeli Defense Forces (IDF) again
invaded South Lebanon to eliminate the PLO. The Israeli invasions of
1978 and 1982 and the subsequent occupation from 1982 to 1985 gave
the Shia a cause for united opposition.[20]

AMAL, the dominant Shia movement at the time, never sought to
radically reform Lebanon into something far different than what it was.
Sadr's successor and former leader of his AMAL militia, Nabih Berri,[21]
steered AMAL toward a more secular orientation along a nationalist path.
He sought to reform the current Lebanese system, not to destroy it. He
did not seek to establish an Islamic State.[22] In 1982, the schism between
reformists and revolutionaries would split AMAL. In that year, Berri
agreed to participate in the National Salvation Committee in their efforts
to reform the Lebanese social and political systems. An AMAL leader,
Hussein al-Musawi, challenged Berri's leadership over the issues of col-
laboration and reformation. Rather than cooperate with the other war-

ring factions, Musawi and his followers broke away and withdrew to Baalbek in the Bekaa Valley of eastern Lebanon.

The Bekaa Valley lies between the Lebanon Mountains to its west, and the Anti Lebanon Mountains to its east. It is primarily an agricultural area that produces wine, beets, and potatoes. But this valley was a good place for Musawi to base his militant followers for their upcoming emergence into the civil conflict. In addition to producing the mentioned staple crops, the valley was a lawless region in which the government of Lebanon could not operate. Due to its remote location between these two mountain ranges and its traditional resistance to rule from Beirut, the valley was an ideal place for criminal elements to grow poppies, the raw material for heroin, and marijuana, and to produce cocaine from imported materials.[23]

In the Bekaa they formed a more militant Shia organization strongly influenced by Khomeini's Iran and committed to the creation of an Islamic state in Lebanon. They called this group Islamic AMAL.[24] Iran, a sponsor of Berri's AMAL, was not happy with the more secular direction that he was pursuing. They wanted a more militant organization whose resources they could tap. They needed fervently religious Shia young men who were disenchanted with the direction Berri was taking his followers. The timing of the 1982 Israeli invasion could not have suited Iran much better. Many leading Shia Lebanese clerics were attending the annual Islamic Conference in Tehran when IDF tanks rolled across the border. Money and Iranian Pasdaran (IRGC agents) followed the clerics back into Lebanon.[25]

The State's Support of One Side

Iran had a stake in the outcome of the conflict in Lebanon. Iran is one of the few Muslim-dominated countries where Shia Muslims outnumber Sunnis. The Iranian Shia Muslims sought to support the Shia population being suppressed in Lebanon. They also saw the conflict as an opportunity to exert their influence over a regional neighbor and counter the growing regional influence of the United States.

On 6 June 1982, in an attempt to deprive Palestinian guerrilla groups of their bases in Southern Lebanon (as well as in reaction to the Abu Nidal assassination attempt on the Israeli Ambassador to London), the Israelis invaded Lebanon. The invasion, led by 70,000 members of the

IDF, was marked by a destructive and brutal occupation.[26] This invasion triggered Iran to act:

> Although Iran never constituted part of Israel's ill-fated plan, the move-
> ment across the borders of the western-armed and -supported Zionist
> state that had usurped Jerusalem from the Muslims roused the passions
> of Khomeini and the political clerics. As a result, Lebanon . . . became
> the field on which the Islamic Revolution would again confront the
> West.[27]

The dominant Shia militia at the time of the invasion was AMAL, a fairly secular and moderate group. At first, the Shia welcomed the Israelis. They were freeing them from the heavy-handed Palestinians who had terrorized their villages and population for years. However, their attitude towards the occupation slowly changed as it became apparent that the Israelis were reluctant to leave after achieving their main objective of driving the PLO from the south.[28]

The newly formed Islamic Republic felt a strong responsibility towards Muslims everywhere. The clerics believed it was their place to face down the Western powers that were supporting what they viewed as repressive regimes in the Middle East. The following quote is from the minutes of a meeting at the Ministry of Islamic Guidance called by the Minister, Seyed Mohammed Khatami, on behalf of Ayatollah Imam Khomeini in May 1984: "[W]e have a heavy duty towards Islam and as such we must prepare ourselves to face the challenges of any enemy . . . and we have liberated all Islamic countries from the yoke of corrupt and reactionary rulers."[29]

Egypt, Saudi Arabia, and Jordan were blaming the United States for not restraining the IDF during the 1982 invasion. The United States was worried that the Soviet Union would come to the aid of its long-time ally, Syria, and intervene in the war. On 25 August 1982, the United States dispatched 800 Marines to Beirut at the head of a Multi-National Force (MNF). The 30-day mission of the MNF was to protect the withdrawal of the battered PLO from Beirut, who were being asked to leave at the behest of the Arab states. Their second mission was to oversee the departure from Lebanon of Syrian Army units. Under this departure plan, the United States gave assurances that the Palestinians left behind in refugee camps would be protected from the Israelis. Later that month, the PLO left Beirut and the Israelis withdrew to Southern Lebanon.[30] The Marines left prior to their self-imposed 30-day deadline with a feeling of "mission accomplished." But, "Khomeini and the hard-liners grabbed hold of the MNF as another military and cultural invasion of the Muslim world, a repetition of the American intrusion into Iran during the shah's era."[31] Iran would not let this lie.

In September the short-lived peace unraveled. On the 14th, just a few days after the US Marines left, President Bashir Gemayel of Lebanon, was assassinated. His assassins had hidden a bomb at his headquarters. Gemayel's election had been supported by Israel. His election was the fulfillment of one of their goals; the establishment of a friendly, Christian government in Lebanon. His brother, Amin, replaced him. The Israelis moved back into West Beirut taking Gemayel's Phalangist militia along with them.[32] On the 16th, with Israel's internal intelligence service Shin Bet watching, Christian Phalangists and Lebanese Maronites sought retribution for the assassination of their Christian President. This splinter group of Christian militiamen massacred over 800 Palestinian women, children, and men too old to fight in the war left behind in the Sabra and Shatilla refugee camps.[33] Over one-quarter of those killed in the camps were Shiites.[34] By the end of the month, 1,500 Marines returned at the head of a new multi-national peace keeping force with a vague and open-ended mission to establish an environment that would permit the Lebanese armed forces to carry out their responsibilities and oversee the withdrawal of all foreign forces from Lebanon.[35]

Notes

1. Raymond Millen, "The Hobbesian Notion of Self-Preservation Concerning Human Behavior during an Insurgency," *Parameters*, XXXVI, 4 (Winter 2006-07): 7.

2. Hala Jaber, *Hezbollah; Born With a Vengeance* (New York: Columbia University Press, 1997) 9.

3. Tom Diaz and Barbara Newman, *Lightning Out of Lebanon; Hezbollah Terrorists on American Soil* (New York: Ballantine Books, 2005) 39.

4. Thomas W. Shreeve, Col (USMCR), *Experiences To Go: Teaching With Intelligence Case Studies; Discussion Paper Number Twelve* (Washington D.C.: Joint Military Intelligence College, 2004) 24.

5. James J. F. Forest, *Teaching Terror; Strategic and Tactical Learning in the Terrorist World* (New York: Rowman and Littlefield Publishers, 2006) 81.

6. Sandra Mackey, *The Iranians* (New York: Penguin Group, 1998) 313.

7. Mackey, 313.

8. John L. Esposito, *The Islamic Threat; Myth or Reality, Third Edition* (New York: Oxford University Press, 1999) 149.

9. Amal Saad-Ghorayeb, *Hizbu'llah: Politics and Religion* (London: Pluto Press, 2002) 26.

10. Diaz and Newman, 49.

11. Jaber, 145-146.

12. Jaber, 10-12.

13. Diaz and Newman, 48.

14. Forest, 81-84.

15. Diaz and Newman, 46.

16. Esposito, 150-151.

17. "The Imam Musa Sadr," *Al Mashriq*, 21 April 1998, URL: < http://almashriq.hiof.no/lebanon/300/320/324.2/musa-sadr >, accessed 4 December 2004.

18. Jaber, 12.

19. Diaz and Newman, 50-51.

20. Esposito, 152.

21. Diaz and Newman, 51.

22. Esposito, 153.

23. Diaz and Newman, 36.

24. Esposito, 154-155.

25. Diaz and Newman, 53.

26. Shreeve, 24.

27. Mackey, 313.

28. Jaber, 14-15.

29. Uri Ra'anan, Robert L. Pfaltzgraff, Jr., Richard H. Schultz, Ernst Halperin, and Igor Lukes, *Hydra of Carnage; International Linkages of Terrorism, The Witnesses Speak* (Lexington, Massachusetts: Lexington Books, 1986) 480-484.

30. Shreeve, 25.

31. Mackey, 315.

32. Jaber, 77.

33. Shreeve, 31.

34. Saad-Ghorayeb, 11.

35. Shreeve, 27.

Chapter 2

Creation of the Surrogate Group

Iran helped create and then provided guidance and material assistance to Lebanese Hizballah (hereafter referred to simply as *Hizballah*) to influence events in Lebanon during its Civil War and to counter US strength in the Persian Gulf region. While Hizballah is still an effective force today, to some degree its reason for existence has changed.

There are nine things that a state sponsor of terrorism must do in order to create a surrogate organization. First, it must infiltrate its own agents, people that can be trusted and directed. Second, the state may need to get logistical assistance or at least acquiescence from a third country. Third, the state needs the support of local leaders sympathetic to its cause. Fourth, it must mobilize local insurgent or resistance fighters. The leaders that the state recruits will be better able to enlist and organize these fighters. Fifth, the state needs to form an umbrella group to absorb fighters from other insurgent, terrorist, and resistance groups and to swell the ranks of their main group. Sixth, the state needs to organize the group. Once the core of the terrorist group is formed, the state will need to mold it into a formidable force. The seventh thing it must do is to train and equip its guerrilla and terrorist fighters. The eighth thing is to fund the group. Finally, the state's surrogate group will need to gain legitimacy in the eyes of the local population by fighting a fierce resistance campaign in the name of the local people. Legitimacy will help the surrogate maintain and expand its membership.

Infiltration by State Agents

Because of the spiritual domination of the Shia Muslim clerics in Iran, much of the world's Shia Muslim population looks to the clerics in Tehran and Qom for guidance and leadership. The Lebanese Shia were no exception. But in order for a movement to become an organized resistance force or operational terrorist group, the Lebanese Shia needed leaders on the ground at their localities to carry out operations and mobilize the populace. In the case of Iran, spiritual guidance and funding from abroad proved insufficient to organize a group and keep it under the state's influence. Frustrated by their ongoing emasculation during this time of crisis in the Lebanese Civil War, the Shia looked to Iran for assistance.

During the Lebanese Civil War, Iran infiltrated its agents into the area to begin the process of starting a surrogate terrorist or militant resistance group and to begin to exert its influence. In order for Hizballah to become an organized resistance force and operational terrorist group, Iran needed allies on the ground in Lebanon to assist in carrying out operations and mobilizing the populace. To achieve this, it first needed to place trusted individuals whom Iran could direct on the ground to begin organizing the different factions, fighters, and prominent figures.

On 12 June 1982, a 1,500-man contingent of the Iranian's Revolutionary Guard Corps (IRGC), or Pasdaran, arrived in the Bekaa Valley, thus becoming the first foreign military expedition of the Islamic Republic.[1] They took many prominent figures from the ranks of the Lebanese Shia Islamic AMAL, and placed them in charge of Hizballah. From the highest levels of Iran's cleric-led government, they knew that they must increase their presence in Lebanon or lose sway to outside influences. Throughout the early 1980s, Iran would continue to infiltrate their agents into the fight. At that same meeting mentioned earlier at the Ministry of Islamic Guidance in 1984, the Minister stated:

> it is not possible for us to confront this enormous force that is supported by the super powers . . . it has been decided that the strike force which at present is composed of a few groups of 10-20 people each, who are currently serving in the Lebanon, should be increased to the size of a brigade . . . formed under the aegis of either the Revolutionary Guards or the Armed Forces . . . we have at present a number of dedicated groups who are ready for action and who have, to the outside world become known as suicide groups . . . are by themselves

inadequate . . . this brigade is for carrying out unconventional warfare in enemy territory.[2]

There were two Iranian agents of note in the beginning of the Pasdaran infiltration. Feridoun Mehdi-Nezhad and Hossein Mosleh, both IRGC Special Forces agents and members of the Pasdaran, conducted numerous operations in Lebanon for over a decade. In the early 1980s, they were assigned to Baalbek, Lebanon, after the Israeli invasion and during the time Western hostages were being held at the Shaykh Abdallah Barracks in the Bekaa Valley. At this time, Mosleh is believed to have organized the Islamic Jihad Organization (IJO) operating in Lebanon but modeled after the Palestinian Fatah's Black September in order to hide Iranian involvement in activities. Also, these two coordinated with IJO and Pasdaran agents to release French hostages Roger Auque and Jean-Louis Normandin. Although unknown at the time, information discovered later indicated IJO was the terrorist wing of Iran's surrogate, Hizballah.[3] In this capacity the IJO was active with Hizballah throughout the 1980s. In 1985, Mehdi-Nezhad and Mosleh held meetings with IJO leader Imad Mughniyah's people preceding the hijacking of TWA flight 847. Mehdi-Nezhad also showed up in the chronicles surrounding the investigation of Pan Am flight 103 that exploded over Lockerbie, Scotland. In 1989, Mehdi-Nezhad and Mosleh led an Iranian hit team to Vienna, Austria to assassinate a Kurdish leader.[4]

Possible Need for Cooperation From a Third Country

If the country the state wishes to influence is not located on its border, the state sponsor of terrorism will need to get at least some assistance from other countries that share borders with the states involved. In seeking to influence the outcome of the Lebanese Civil War, Iran needed a neighboring state's assistance, namely Syria. At the time, Syria already had a strong presence in Lebanon and knew the landscape and culture well because of years of intervention in Lebanese domestic affairs. Thus, Iran sought to get assistance from Syria in order to infiltrate Lebanon.

Syrian cooperation with Iran to use Hizballah as a surrogate in regional conflicts, mainly with Israel, has always been more out of practicality rather than ideological fervor. Hafez al-Assad, who seized power in Syria in 1970 after the first military coup by the Alawite-dominated military in 1966, would, throughout his rule of Syria, align himself with Iran out of a desire to maintain his regime.[5]

Syria and Iran are not completely without cultural ties that would justify a bond between the two. However, this bond is more between the Shia in Iran and the religious minority that accounts for only 11% of the population, that being the Alawites. Alawi is a mix of Phoenician paganism, Greek astrology, eastern reincarnationism, and Christianity that grew out of the mountains of northwest Syria. They would later incorporate Shia Islam into their belief system. This sect was branded heretical by mainstream Islam and its members persecuted for centuries. It wasn't until a fatwa (religious decree) in 1973 by Lebanese Shia cleric Imam Sayyed Musa as-Sadr (founder of AMAL) declared Alawi a sect of Shia Islam, that the Alawites were granted some legitimacy. This fatwa was a maneuver by the Alawites to counter the growing threat of Sunni fundamentalism.[6]

Syria's alliances with Iran and Hizballah can also be seen as their way of checking the power of their regional enemies. In the 1967 war, Israel captured the Golan Heights in the region that borders Syria, Lebanon, Israel, and Jordan. Since that war, the contested area has been a battleground between Israel and Syria. Syria uses Hizballah to keep Israel off balance while avoiding direct confrontation with a superior military. Syria has also used their ties to Iran to counter Iraqi strength. During the Iran-Iraq War of 1980-88, Hafaz al-Assad believed the time was right to cripple his stronger neighbor (Iraq) and align himself with Iran.[7]

In November 1982, local press reported that the Islamic AMAL leader, Hussein al-Musawi seized the Shaykh Abdallah Barracks in Baalbek in the Bekaa Valley from Syrian Gendarmerie. The Syrians, who occupied the barracks since their intervention in the Lebanese Civil War in 1976, facilitated this transfer to the IRGC.[8] Syrian consent was critical to Iran's creation of Hizballah as it gave the Iranian Pasdaran unfettered access to the Bekaa Valley and access to Lebanon's borders. Iran capitalized on this and dispatched 1,500 Pasdaran agents to help build an extensive military network in Baalbek, Shia neighborhoods in Southern Lebanon, and West Beirut.[9] Baalbek would be their main base of operations. It was not under Israeli occupation and was physically close to Syria. This area provided the IRGC with a safe haven in which to work and organize their movement as well as a corridor to Iran.[10]

In order to get equipment into Lebanon, Iran would have to ship material in by air, sea, or land. Syrian help was instrumental with the transfer of equipment via a land route across the Syrian border and cargo flights via the Damascus International Airport.

The Iranian Embassy in Damascus became the center for organizing and coordinating Iranian support for Hizballah from the beginning.[11] Damascus has remained a center from where Syria and Iran, through Hizballah, influence, control, and direct the terrorist activities of not only Hizballah, but also the Palestinian HAMAS, the Palestinian Islamic Jihad (PIJ), and the Popular Front for the Liberation of Palestine-General Command (PFLP-GC).[12]

Syria was finally induced to withdraw its forces from Lebanon in April 2005. The pressure to leave Lebanon came from the United Nations following the assassination of former Lebanese Prime Minister Rafik Hariri. Hariri was a proponent of United Nations Security Council (UNSC) Resolution 1559 calling for Syrian withdrawal from Lebanon and an end to their interference in Lebanese affairs. The UN investigation found evidence that pointed conclusively to involvement of both Syrian and Lebanese officials. This was seen as the beginning of a new era for Lebanon. However, according to a UN report issued October 2005, Hizbollah was still receiving arms from Iran, and the equipment was still being "transported through Syria with no apparent Syrian objection."[13]

Use of Existing Local Leaders

The state wishing to create a surrogate group must support local community leaders that are already in place, or ready to be placed back into the area from exile, that have great influence among the local population. The leaders the state sponsor chooses could be members of existing movements. They could be civic, political and/or religious leaders. These leaders should be adherents of the ideology or religion the state wishes to exploit so they will be easier to manipulate. The leaders from the state sponsoring the surrogate will help mobilize the sympathetic population through civic, charitable and social networks, political activism, and armed resistance. Iran took many prominent figures from the ranks of the Lebanese Islamic militant group, Islamic AMAL, and placed them in charge of Hizballah.

There are a few individuals influential throughout the formation and life of Hizballah that should be elaborated on. The most notorious was Imad Fa'iz Mughniyah. He was a Shiite from southern Lebanon. Born on 12 July 1962 in Tayr Dibba, a village in the mountains above Tyre, he is believed to have grown up in the slums of Ayn ad-Dilbah in southern Beirut. He was a teenager when the civil war began.[14] At age fourteen he joined Yassir Arafat's elite personal security service in Fatah, Force 17, as a bodyguard for Arafat from 1976 to 1982.[15] Later he joined Hizballah at the encouragement of Lebanese Shiite spiritual leader Muhammad Husayn Fadlallah, for whom he was a bodyguard after serving in Fatah, when Hizballah was formed in 1982.

Before the terrorist attacks of 11 September 2001, he was responsible for the murder of more Americans than any other terrorist in the world. Mughniyah was responsible for the kidnappings of Central Intelligence Agency (CIA) Beirut Station Chief Bill Buckley and CNN Bureau Chief Jeremy Levin, as well as two French clerics, Laurence Martin Jenco and Benjamin Weir. He was indicted by the US Department of Justice as the mastermind behind the hijacking of TWA flight 847 that was diverted from Athens, Greece to Beirut. During this hijacking, he murdered US Navy Diver Robert Stethem aboard the plane.[16] Several of the hostages from that flight were handed over to AMAL while four went to the IJO.[17] Not only is the 1985 abduction, torture, and murder of Buckley and the hijacking of TWA Flight 847, attributed to Mughniyah, but he is also believed to be the mastermind behind the April 1983 bombing of the US Embassy, the 1983 bombing of the US Marine Barracks, and the 1984 bombing of the US Embassy Annex, all in Beirut.[18] Until his assassination in Damascus in February 2008, he was the Chief of Hizballah Security, which is thought to be the nom de guerre of the IJO. Mughniyah was generally believed by Western intelligence services "to work directly under Iranian intelligence and to use a small circle of trusted Lebanese Shia to carry out the instructions of hardliners in Tehran."[19] He had a personal unit of 100-150 men at his disposal called the Islamic Jihad Organization (IJO).[20]

As-Sayyid Hassan Nasrallah is the current Secretary General of Hizballah. He is a prominent Shia cleric from Lebanon who joined AMAL in the 1970s. He left AMAL in 1982 and helped form Hizballah because he felt AMAL's reaction to the Israeli invasion of Lebanon was too soft. Nasrallah had many followers within AMAL who were willing to defect because they believed AMAL was not reacting to the invasion with enough ferocity. He is very popular among the Iranian leadership and has close religious ties to its clerics. He is also very popular among the Hizballah rank-and-file because he has eschewed a corrupt and lavish lifestyle. Nasrallah has led the Consultative Council (Hizballah's highest governing body) as Secretary General since 1992, when his predecessor, Abbas Musawi was killed by the IDF.[21] He oversaw the party's later integration into Lebanese politics and helped steer them towards political prominence. He accentuates the themes of Christian-Muslim reconciliation and co-existence in Lebanon's political pluralist society.[22]

Lastly, Muhammad Husayn Fadlallah is the spiritual guide for Hizballah but is not officially associated with the group and never joined the party. Fadlallah was born in 1935 and was educated in Najaf, Iraq. His family is from Lebanon and he returned to Beirut in 1966.[23] He was the chief mujtahid, or arbiter of Islamic law, for the Shia community in Southern Lebanon and was their most prominent Shia cleric when Hizballah was formed in 1982.[24] The ruling Iranian clerics favored Fadlallah because he provided them with a sympathetic leader with an authentic Lebanese clerical base.[25] He has always been sympathetic to Hizballah's ideals. By not officially joining the party but preaching its tenets to the local Shiite population, he served Iran as a spiritual spokesman that could not be blamed for Hizballah's guerrilla activity or acts of terrorism.

Use of Existing Local Fighters

The leaders mentioned above can serve to mobilize a group of people the state needs to carry out a resistance, insurgency, or terrorist campaign. Local leaders can supply the movement with willing combatants, guerrillas and terrorists. These operatives can be sympathetic to the state's message or at least willing to follow their local leader in whichever direction he leads them.

Hizballah was formed in the early 1980s in the Shia neighborhoods of Southern Lebanon, the Bekaa Valley, and Beirut. It received support in many different forms from the Shia Muslim theocratic state of Iran. Hizballah's guerrilla soldiers, terrorists, politicians, social workers, and supporters have been made up largely of Shia Muslims from Lebanon. Support for Hizballah was galvanized in the early 1980s in Southern Lebanon. The invasion by Israeli forces and the subsequent occupation made it easier for Iran to attract Lebanese to the cause of resistance to an occupying force and to join Hizballah.

Iran and Hizballah have been able to work closely together mainly because of shared Shia Islamic beliefs. Hizballah's members have been willing to work with Iran's specialists that are sent to the region to train and organize the surrogates. Much of the draw to Hizballah from other Shia groups such as AMAL and Islamic AMAL can be attributed to the training provided by the IRGC in the early 1980s. This is evidenced in Islamic AMAL leader Musawi's own writing about the IRGC camps and the indoctrination that took place. In the beginning, most of the key operatives were drawn from Musawi's own militia which served him during the years prior to the 1982 Israeli invasion.[26] Training took place in camps in the Bekaa Valley and in Iran.

Formation of an Umbrella Group

In Lebanon, Iran initially wanted to use an existing Shia movement like AMAL to increase its control over events and to limit US influence there. When AMAL would not follow Iran's direction, Iran patiently began to organize a myriad of resistance groups more inclined to pursue its own goals. Iran's future surrogate, Hizballah, "provided the umbrella under which cells formed in local mosques gathered."[27] Rather than a structured organization, it linked a panoply of Islamic groups who looked to Iran for ideological inspiration as well as financial and operational help. Eventually, these groups would organize into a single organizational framework and form Iran's surrogate. By the mid-1980s Hizballah encompassed a number of revolutionary groups all with a common outlook and agenda: the dismantling of the Lebanese state and the creation of an Islamic one. Some of the groups included Islamic AMAL, Jund Allah, the Hussein Death Squad, the Revolutionary Justice Organization, and al-Jihad.[28] Most of the Hizballah cadre came from Islamic AMAL and were brought over by Hizballah's spiritual leader, Lebanese cleric Fadlallah.[29]

Foreign intervention and Israeli brutality further encouraged cooperation among the umbrella movement members. The initial Israeli invasion in June 1982 generated spontaneous resistance as well. Hostility towards Israel was further inflamed by Israeli forces desecration of the Ashura ceremonial procession in 1983 in Nabatiyyeh, an important Shia event.[30]

Other things aided the formation of Hizballah. There was a split within AMAL over the primacy they placed on involvement in the political process in Lebanon. Some AMAL members did not want to be involved in a non-Islamic, secular government. They "expressed the criticisms of many Shi'ite clerics to AMAL's moderate position and readiness to integrate into the existing Lebanese order."[31] The under-representation of Shiites in the Maronite dominated Parliament of Lebanon propelled some Lebanese Shiites towards political action and some towards militant resistance.

Organization of the Group

Once the state sponsoring the terrorist organization has the group's leadership in place and its militants ready to carry out guerrilla or terrorist activities, a number of supporting activities must take place to ensure operational continuance. The organization must develop a governing structure with the assistance of the state sponsor. They must also develop a purpose that their followers can rally behind and that is acceptable to their sponsor.

The following information is from an open letter from Hizballah in April 1984, obtained from the Joint Publications Research Service, *Near East/South Asia Report*. This letter essentially served as an operational charter outlining Hizballah's purpose, goals, and methods. In the letter, Hizballah emphatically states that it is directly linked to and receives guidance from Khomeini's Iran. They also openly claim responsibility for acts of terrorism including the bombing of the US Marine Barracks in Beirut. Hizballah outlines its list of enemies including the United States, France, NATO, and at the forefront, Israel. The letter further states:

> Our sons are in a state of ever-escalating confrontation against these enemies until the following objectives are achieved . . . Israel's final departure from Lebanon as a prelude to its final obliteration from existence and the liberation of venerable Jerusalem from the talons of occupation . . . The final departure of America, France, and their allies from Lebanon.[32]

The letter goes on to state that they believe Israel is the "American spearhead in our Islamic world." They also warn other countries not yet involved in the Middle East's conflicts "against being dragged into serving American interests at the expense of our nation's freedom and interest."[33] Hizballah's sentiment towards Iranian dominance was further emphasized by Hizballah spokesman Sheikh Ibrahim al-Amin on 16 February 1985. In this public declaration, he stated that Hizballah abides "by the orders of a wise and just command currently embodied in the supreme exemplar of Ayatollah Khomeini."[34]

Once the group has a purpose and followers, it must be organized into an effective body. The central governing structure of Hizballah was broken down into three components: the Shura (Executive) Council, the military wing or the Islamic Resistance, and the intelligence and security departments. The Majlis ash-Shura, or Consultative Council, governs the political apparatus. There is a fair degree of institutional autonomy characterizing the party's political wing.[35] The Shura Council elects a Secretary General. While the Secretary General and the Shura Council do not get involved in the day-to-day activities, they are ultimately responsible for determining Hizballah's overall strategy. The General Convention is the body that implements Shura Council orders and plans day-to-day operations. The Politburo provides advice to the Shura.

The military wing, or the Islamic Resistance, is organized by regional commands centered on Beirut, the Bekaa Valley, and Southern Lebanon. This wing is directly responsible to the military committee of the Shura. The Amn al-Hizb (the "Party's Security") protects Hizballah leaders, preserves discipline and monitors all levels of Hizballah's hierarchy, including the Consultative Council.[36]

Training of and Equipping the Group

The state must also train and equip a group of people willing to do the fighting for it. This group will carry out the guerrilla attacks, kidnappings, and suicide missions ostensibly in the name of the organization, but ultimately at the behest of the state sponsor. According to a RAND study on organizational learning in terrorist groups, Hizballah "apparently had a two-track training program: It trained everyday fighters in its own camps and incorporated lessons learned from its skirmishes with Israel, but it also sent elite troops to Iran for specialized training.[37] Hizballah's main training camp in the Bekaa Valley is located at Janba, while another major facility is located at Wadi Mnaira.[38]

Successful tactics employed by Hizballah included ambushes of IDF and South Lebanese Army (SLA) small unit foot patrols, entrapment scenarios, and multiple improvised explosive device (IED) arrays. Hizballah's arsenal that is supplied by Iran includes assault rifles, rocket-propelled grenades, anti-tank missiles, mortars, and man-portable air defense systems. Hizballah has also been able to acquire TOW missiles from Iran. The BGM-71 TOW (tube-launched, optically tracked, wire-guided) missiles had probably come from Iran via Damascus, along with some initial training.[39]

Funding of the Group

Money must be channeled to the terrorists to fund operations or to the guerrilla fighters who need to pay its soldiers and buy weapons and equipment. If the state sponsor wishes to maintain plausible deniability with regards to its support for terrorism, the transfer of funds must be done covertly.

While it is almost absolutely certain (because it is never admitted) that Iran provides military goods and services as well as financial aid to Hizballah, a specific dollar amount of aid is not known. However, some experts put the annual worth in real-world terms at $25-50 million.[40] The chief conduit of funds in the beginning of the relationship between Hizballah and Iran was the Iranian Embassy in Damascus and Iranian Ambassador Hojjatoleslam Ali Akbar Mohtashemi.[41]

Legitimacy Gained through Resistance

The state sponsored surrogate group will need to gain legitimacy in the eyes of the local population by fighting a fierce resistance campaign consisting of militant activity and acts of terror against the perceived occupiers or oppressors. Legitimacy in the eyes of the local population will help the group maintain and expand its membership and continue to distract attention from the state sponsor.

In May 2000, after eighteen years of fighting a terror and guerrilla campaign against the Israelis in Southern Lebanon, Israel withdrew. The only lands retained by Israel were the sparsely populated Shebaa Farms. Hizballah was formed with Iranian assistance mainly as a resistance movement to Israeli occupation of Southern Lebanon. They expanded and received support primarily because they were a guerrilla force fighting the Israeli occupiers.

However, the conflict over the disputed area continues. In Hizballah's view, Israel still occupies part of Lebanese sovereign territory.

Israeli seizure of the Golan Heights from Syria during the 1967 Six Day War included the seizure of the Shebaa Farms as well. When Israeli forces withdrew in May 2000, Israeli forces remained in Shebaa,

considering it part of annexed Syrian territory. However, Hezbollah
and the Lebanese and the Syrian governments claim that Shebaa be-
longs to Lebanon, arguing that the Syrian government gave the territory to Lebanon in 1951.[42]

The constant state of conflict between Israel and her neighbors has the
ever-present potential to escalate into something more than border skirmishes. In the 1990s, Israel tried to eliminate their nemesis, Hizballah,
only to see their plans backfire. Operation Accountability in 1993 and
Operation Grapes of Wrath in 1996 had the stated operational goals of
wiping out Hizballah bases in the south of Lebanon. Their unstated strategic goals, according to an Israeli economist, seemed to be the disruption of the Lebanese economy and the restraint of their economic rival as
the entryway to the Near East. In the 1990s, Lebanon was rebuilding and
attracting foreign investors. Israel had signed peace agreements with the
Palestinians as well as some of its neighbors. Economic competition between the neighbors was on the rise.[43]

In both Operations, the IDF sought to achieve their goals using artillery, air and sea attacks. They did not want a repeat of the 1982 ground
invasion thus incurring similar casualties. After both Operations, Hizballah
emerged damaged but more popular. The Israeli offenses sought to alienate
the Lebanese people from Hizballah in the hope of ending support for
them. However, it actually served to bring the people closer to Hizballah.
Many Lebanese saw Hizballah as the only body determined to fight the
occupation and able to challenge the might of the region's superpower.[44]

The Israelis did not learn strategic lessons from their attempts to
eradicate Hizballah in the 1990s. An example of this was the Israeli-
Hizballah war in the summer of 2006. "The timing of the group's
[Hizballah's] action on this particular occasion had probably more to do
with the emerging confrontation in Gaza between Israel and Palestinian
militants than with any enticements from Tehran."[45] Hizballah launched
a raid into northern Israel and captured two Israeli soldiers while the
situation was heating up on Israel's southern flank with Palestinian militants in Gaza. Israel's stated strategic objectives were to stop the firing
of Katyusha rockets against Israeli communities from southern Lebanon
and to return the two abducted soldiers.[46] However, Israel had loftier
goals. They sought to eradicate Hizballah through the application of overwhelming military force and a fierce air campaign. After thirty-four days
of fighting, Israel had not achieved a decisive victory nor had they res-

cued their captured soldiers, and a cease-fire was adopted. Hizballah fighters sustained the fight against the Middle East's most powerful military and achieved an Israeli withdrawal.[47] Israel would not stay in Lebanon as it had done in the past. After eighteen years of fighting a guerrilla war before the close of the last century, Israel had conceded that remaining in Lebanon to hunt down their elusive enemy was not worth the sacrifice. Secretary General Nasrallah declared it a strategic, historic victory over Israel for Hizballah.

As a result, the popularity of Hizballah and its prime supporter, Iran, in the Arab and Muslim worlds rose markedly. The real loser in the conflict was Lebanon. After the thirty-four-day campaign, a proxy fight once again decimated the state of Lebanon. Over 1,200 civilians were killed, 130,000 homes were destroyed, and an estimated $7 billion in damages sustained.[48]

Despite the destruction caused to Lebanon by the constant skirmishes and larger-scale military conflicts between Israel and Hizballah, Lebanon still allows Hizballah to conduct hostile operations along the Blue Line on the premise of a legitimate resistance to the occupation of Lebanon. The Lebanese government has even gone as far as exempting Hizballah from money laundering and terrorism financing laws by designating the organization a "legal resistance" group in February 2006. But even prior to this official recognition, the Lebanese mission to the UN during Operation Grapes of Wrath defended Hizballah's right to exist before the world. The mission stated that the Lebanese government was not prepared to take action against Hizballah while Israeli troops were still occupying South Lebanon.[49]

There could be many reasons for this acceptance of Hizballah. The Lebanese government could be acting in its own interest to preserve the fragile political structure by avoiding a political crisis. Hizballah as a political organization is powerful and gaining strength, especially in the Shia-dominated areas of Beirut, southern Lebanon, and the Bekaa Valley. The Lebanese government may also be trying to avoid a military crisis with an experienced, well-equipped, well-financed military force with powerful regional backers. Lebanon has stated that it will abide by its international obligations, including UNSCR 1559, which calls for the "disarming and disbanding of all Lebanese and non-Lebanese militias." But they have avoided trying to disarm them by designating Hizballah a legitimate resistance group.[50]

Practicality and regime survival may not be the only reasons for
Lebanon's tolerance of the constant state of war that exists because of
Hizballah's presence on their soil. The Lebanese military is not in a
position to face Hizballah in a civil war. The far superior Israeli Defense
Forces have not been able to crush Hizballah in any of the small and
medium-scale conflicts. The Lebanese army's chances of accomplishing
what the IDF could not do on repeated attempts are quite slim. Nor could
Lebanon face the IDF in conventional war. Therefore, if they cannot
defeat Hizballah, they might as well use them, if Hizballah's intentions
are to continue to resist Israeli attempts at regional influence. While
Hizballah is not allowed, either by their host or their sponsors, to do
whatever it wants, they still have "more flexibility to fight against Israel
in ways that states such as Syria, Lebanon, and Iran do not have."[51]

Notes

1. Sandra Mackey, *The Iranians* (New York: Penguin Group, 1998) 314.
2. Uri Ra'anan, Robert L. Pfaltzgraff, Jr., Richard H. Schultz, Ernst
Halperin, and Igor Lukes, *Hydra of Carnage; International Linkages of Terrorism, The Witnesses Speak* (Lexington, Massachusetts: Lexington Books, 1986)
480-484.
3. Robert Baer, *See No Evil* (New York: Crown Publishers, 2002) 262.
4. Baer, 262.
5. Pat Proctor, "The Mythical Shia Crescent," *Parameters*, XXXVIII, 1
(Spring 2008), 35.
6. Pat Proctor, 35-36.
7. Pat Proctor, 36-39.
8. Baer, 73.
9. Amal Saad-Ghorayeb, *Hizbu'llah: Politics and Religion* (London: Pluto
Press, 2002) 14.
10. Hala Jaber, *Hezbollah; Born With a Vengeance* (New York: Columbia
University Press, 1997) 51.
11. John L. Esposito, *The Islamic Threat; Myth or Reality, Third Edition*
(New York: Oxford University Press, 1999) 155.
12. Rachel Ehrenfeld, *Funding Evil; How Terrorism is Financed-and How
to Stop It* (Los Angeles: Bonus Books, 2003) 131.
13. Anthony H. Cordesman, "Lebanese Security and Hezbollah," *Center
for Strategic and International Studies: Arleigh A. Burke Chair in Strategy*
(Washington DC, working draft revised 14 July 2006) 2-5.

14. Tom Diaz and Barbara Newman, *Lightning Out of Lebanon; Hezbollah Terrorists on American Soil* (New York: Ballantine Books, 2005) 62-63.

15. Ehrenfeld, 121.

16. Diaz and Newman, 66.

17. Baer, 92-98.

18. Ehrenfeld, 121.

19. "Hizballah in the Firing Line," *Middle East Report OnLine*, 28 April 2002, URL: < http://www.merip.org/mero/mero042803.html >, accessed 17 September 2004.

20. Diaz and Newman, 64.

21. Ehrenfeld, 123.

22. Saad-Ghorayeb, 2.

23. Diaz and Newman, 52.

24. Esposito, 156-157.

25. Diaz and Newman, 53.

26. Brian A. Jackson, John C. Baker, Kim Cragin, John Parachini, Horacio R. Trujillo, and Peter Chalk, *Aptitude For Destruction; Volume 2, Case Studies of Organizational Learning in Five Terrorist Groups* (Santa Monica, Ca.: RAND Corporation, 2005) 44.

27. Mackey, 314.

28. Esposito, 156.

29. Saad-Ghorayeb, 15.

30. Saad-Ghorayeb, 11.

31. "Hizballah: New Course or Continued Warfare," *Middle East Review of International Affairs*, September 2000, 4, 3. URL: < http://meria.idc.ac.il/journal/2000/issue3/jv4n3a3.html >, accessed 21 August 2004.

32. Ra'anan, 488-491.

33. Ibid.

34. Jaber, 54.

35. Saad-Ghorayeb, 117.

36. Cordesman, "Lebanese Security and Hezbollah," 21.

37. Jackson, 48.

38. *GlobalSecurity.org*, "The Training of Terrorist Organizations," URL: < http://www.globalsecurity.org/military/library/report/1995/SDE.htm >, accessed on 7 August 2009.

39. Jackson, 49.

40. Anthony H. Cordesman, "Iran's Support of the Hezbollah in Lebanon," (*Center for Strategic and International Studies: Arleigh A. Burke Chair in Strategy*, Washington DC, 15 July 2006) 3.

41. Jaber, 150.

42. Cordesman, "Lebanese Security and Hezbollah," 23.

43. Jaber, 177.

44. Jaber, 171-178.

45. Ali M. Ansari, *Iran Under Ahmadinejad: The Politics of Confrontation* (The International Institute for Strategic Studies, Adelphi Paper 393, London: Routledge, 2007) 64.

46. Sarah E. Kreps, "The 2006 Lebanon War: Lessons Learned," *Parameters*, XXXVII, 1 (Spring 2007): 75.

47. Gawdat Bahgat, "United States-Iranian Relations: The Terrorism Challenge," *Parameters*, XXXVIII, 4 (Winter 2008-09), 13-14.

48. William K. Mooney, Jr., "Stabilizing Lebanon: Peacekeeping or Nation-Building," *Parameters*, XXXVII, 3 (Autumn 2007): 28.

49. Jaber, 195.

50. Cordesman, "Lebanese Security and Hezbollah," 17-18.

51. Cordesman, "Lebanese Security and Hezbollah," 26.

Chapter 3

Creation of Ambiguity to Avoid Responsibility/Blame

Attempting to hide the relationship between a state sponsor and a terrorist surrogate group by simply denying the existence of the relationship may not be enough to avoid responsibility for the acts of terrorism committed by the surrogate. The adversary that the state sponsor is fighting will be motivated to discover the identity of the perpetrators and their sponsors. The state sponsor must try to confuse and misdirect the intelligence gathering agencies of its enemies in order to protect against the defeat of sensitive operations. This can be accomplished by operating under aliases; denying involvement in terrorism; creating, working with, and funding groups other than your primary surrogate; and marginalizing the neutrality of your adversary in the conflict in the eyes of the parties involved.

Operation Under Alias

The relationship between the state sponsor and terrorist surrogate must be amorphous enough for the state sponsor to be able to deny the relationship to avoid retaliation against it and/or condemnation of its support of terrorism by the international community. However, the relationship must be apparent enough to get the message across to the victims. One way to accomplish this is for the terrorist operations group to operate under aliases.

The militant and terrorist wings of Hizballah operated under different aliases in order to further confuse the situation in Lebanon in the early 1980s. The Islamic Resistance was formed following the Israel invasion of Lebanon in 1982 but did not officially reveal itself as Hizballah's militant wing until 1985. By 1983, fifty terrorist attacks had occurred with a confirmed or suspected Iranian involvement, most in Lebanon where Hizballah operated with direct Iranian support. In order to protect themselves from direct retribution, Hizballah tried to mask these acts under the nom de plume "Islamic Jihad."[1] The name "Islamic Jihad" was chosen by the IRGC to intentionally cast confusion as there were other groups operating in the area at that time that incorporated this description in their name.[2]

The Islamic Jihad Organization (IJO) was claiming responsibility for kidnappings and terrorist acts in 1983, years before it was discovered that it was the terrorist wing of Hizballah.[3] For instance, in March 1985, Terry Anderson, the chief Middle East correspondent for the Associated Press, was abducted. He was held captive until December 1991. In that same month in 1985, Marcel Fontaine, vice consul of the French mission, "was abducted by three men while walking to his office in West Beirut. He was driven away in a car similar to one used in three other kidnappings during the same period." Later on that same day, another French diplomat, Marcel Carton, and an embassy employee, Danielle Perez, had failed to report to work and were reported kidnapped. Islamic Jihad claimed responsibility for all of these, and many other kidnappings in Lebanon.[4]

The IJO was up to other terrorist operations in addition to kidnappings. In the beginning of 1983, fighting between the Druze and Christian militias in Beirut intensified and Israeli casualties increased. A multinational force led by the United States and including Great Britain, France, and Italy patrolled Beirut. During this confusion, Hizballah began attacking US forces. In February 1983, the IJO claimed the first direct attack on a twelve-man US Marine patrol.[5] On a patrol in a community north of the airfield, a grenade was thrown at the Marines resulting in five Marines injured. The opinions of some Lebanese had begun to change regarding the neutrality of the MNF. According to a speech by General Paul X. Kelley, USMC, 29th Commandant of the Marine Corps, about this time several Lebanese factions may have perceived a subtle shift of the US forces from being pro-Lebanese to pro-Christian.[6]

On 18 April 1983, the US Embassy in Beirut was car-bombed. The powerful bomb collapsed the first seven floors of the building. This was the first large-scale attack of a US embassy building anywhere in the

world. Seventeen Americans were killed.[7] The Americans killed constituted a large part of the US intelligence expertise in the area. This attack
was claimed by Islamic Jihad.

In September, following the Embassy attack, the leader of Islamic
AMAL was contacted by an Iranian official and given instructions. The
Iranian official was Hojjatoleslam Ali Akbar Mohtashemi, the Iranian
Ambassador in Damascus. The instructions were to take dramatic action
against the US Marines. Mohtashemi's job was to originate and super-
vise the formation and development of Iranian directed terrorist groups
from his embassy in Syria. After his instructions were conveyed a meeting took place in Baalbek. Present at the meeting was the Iranian chief of
the IRGC in Lebanon, a man named Kanani, and three Lebanese clerics
who were to serve as the Secretaries General of Hizballah: Subhi Tufayli,
Abbas Musawi, and Hassan Nasrallah. The plans were laid for a horrific
terrorist attack against the US Marines with Imad Mughniyah placed in
charge of the operation.[8]

Mughniyah, along with his brother-in-law, Mustapha Youssef
Badreden, took command of the operation. Badreden had been a member
of the ad-Dawa party's militia. The ad-Dawa party was originally an
Iraqi Islamic party that was crushed by Saddam Hussein in the 1970s and
early 1980s. Their ideology sprang from the Shia circle of clerics in
Najaf, Iraq.[9] They watched the Marine's barracks at the Beirut International Airport and knew their routines. They knew that the Marines slept
late on Sundays. They knew what time the vegetable and provision trucks
arrived in the area to deliver goods to the Marines. They also knew what
trucks were used.[10]

The Headquarters of the 24th Marine Amphibious Unit (MAU) was
the Battalion Landing Team (BLT). It was located in a four-story building that had once been the offices of the Lebanese Aviation Administration Bureau located at the Beirut International Airport. This building had
been occupied by the PLO, then the Syrian Army, then the Israelis, and
finally the US Marines. On any given day there were about 350 people
working at the BLT. On Sunday, 23 October, a 19-ton Mercedes Benz
delivery truck driven by an Iranian operative for Hizballah, Ismalal Ascari,
approached the BLT. The Mercedes Benz was similar to trucks used to
deliver water and other supplies to the barracks. At 0622 hours, Ascari's
truck maneuvered around the barriers, rolled through a guardhouse and
exploded in the lobby of the building. Two hundred and forty one people
were killed. The bomb had an explosive force of something between

12,000 and 18,000 pounds of TNT. The bomb was constructed using pentaerythritol tetranitrate (PETN), a commercially manufactured explosive used mostly for military ordinance. Cylinders of propane gas were arrayed around the PETN to enhance its ferocity.[11] This bomb was so large and well constructed that there was widespread speculation at the time that the unknown terrorists had outside expert assistance in preparing the device.[12] Mughniyah and Badreden watched the execution of their plan from the roof of a nearby building.[13] Although this too was claimed by the IJO, there was still confusion as to what group perpetrated the act and to what extent Hizballah was organized at this point. It was alleged at the time that Hussein al-Musawi, the head of Islamic AMAL, as well as a member of the Hizballah Planning Council organized this attack.[14] But that was not commonly known. These examples illustrate the ability of the surrogate to not only confuse the adversary as to who the perpetrator of the act was, but to further mask the involvement of a state sponsor with an agenda behind the scenes.

Denial of Involvement and the Involvement of Your Surrogate

Simply denying involvement in terrorism adds ambiguity to an already ambiguous environment. The opinions of some people, especially sympathetic world leaders, may already be biased in favor of the state sponsor of terrorism and against the powers it is fighting. These people will be more inclined to believe the denials or can at least assist by giving supporting statements.

At the Arab Summit in Cairo, Egypt in 1996, Iran denied its association with the use of terrorism. At the summit, Iranian delegates emphasized the bias of the West's use of the label of terrorist. It said this definition left no room for legitimate national resistance movements and liberation struggles. Iran emphasized its principle opposition to the Israeli-Palestinian peace process. They also claimed they were victims of terrorism at the hands of the Iraqi-based People's Mujahadeen; a group the United States considers a terrorist organization.[15] Furthermore, Iran claimed the United States uses a double standard in its definition of terrorism, specifically, by refusing to categorize undemocratic and repressive Arab regimes that are pro-Israeli and pro-Western as terrorists.[16] Author Saad-Ghorayeb states:

Although no concrete evidence has yet transpired which directly incriminates Hizbu'llah [sic] in the taking of hostages, this has not prevented many observers of contemporary Islamic movements from finding the party culpable for the abduction of over 87, mainly Western, foreigners.[17]

Hizballah has consistently denied any responsibility in kidnappings that took place in the 1980s. However, it is clear that Hizballah "was well aware of the figures behind the kidnappings and knew the details of their enterprises. The group provided safe cover to the kidnappers in areas under its control."[18] In fact, British-Lebanese journalist Hala Jaber, author of *Hezbollah: Born With a Vengeance*, states that the group that claimed many of the kidnappings, Islamic Jihad, was simply a covert name for Hizballah.[19]

Creation, Working With, and Funding Other Groups

For the state sponsor, it helps to add ambiguity to the chaotic situation by creating and influencing a myriad of other militant groups. Other terrorist groups active in the area of conflict tax the resources of intelligence-gathering agencies. By creating and funding other groups to act in the same area and at the same time the state sponsor creates confusion that can hide the main surrogate's activities and the connection to it as a state sponsor. By using this form of active deception, as author Sandra Khalsa explains, the adversary causes an object or situation to seem threatening when in reality the adversary does not have the intention and/or capability to carry out the threat.[20] As a result, the target of the active deception, their adversary intelligence gathering apparatus, focuses their energy and resources in the wrong direction.

These other groups can serve the state's purpose by carrying out guerrilla and terrorist attacks against their target. However, the state cannot let them gain power at the expense of their main surrogate. Iran provided material assistance to other groups in the same way it did Hizballah with funding, organizational support and training. However, none of these entities ever encroached on Hizballah's status. For instance, in 1982, Sheikh Sa'id Sha'ban created the Islamic Unity Movement. He was a Shiite with political ties to Iran through Hizballah. Another group, the Islamic Movement was headed by Sadiq al-Musawi, a cousin of Islamic AMAL's Hussein al-Musawi with direct access to Iranian militants. Other groups such as the Revolutionary Justice Organization and the Oppressed of the Earth Organization served as a cover for Hizballah's militant activities by holding Western hostages. Iran also supported Sunni groups influenced by Hizballah such as the Islamic Struggle Movement, which first appeared in 1987.[21]

Iran has also worked with other Sunni groups adding further confusion to the situation, including Saudi Hizballah and al-Qaeda. On 25 June 1996 at 2200 hours, the Khobar Towers in Dhahran, Saudi Arabia, used to house members of the US Air Force's 4404th Fighter Wing personnel, was truck-bombed. The attack killed nineteen Americans. The bomb was classic Hizballah. A truck was converted to hold 5,000 pounds of TNT. The blast was felt nearly twenty miles away in Bahrain. Iran had sponsored the creation of the Saudi wing of Hizballah to carry out the attack. Hizballah and Iran funded, coordinated, and planned the attack. They recruited the terrorists and trained them in training camps in Lebanon and elsewhere. Hizballah explosives experts stayed at a nearby farm during the two weeks preceding that attack to assist the terrorists with the logistics of the operation. The whole operation was directed by Ali Fallahian, the longtime Iranian Minister of Intelligence.[22]

This attack was blamed not only on Saudi Hizballah, but possibly Usama bin Laden and al-Qaeda.[23] According to then Federal Bureau of Investigation (FBI) Director Louis Freeh, Iran was linked to the attack:

> Over the course of the investigation the evidence became clear that while the attack was staged by Saudi Hezbollah [sic] members, the entire operation was planned, funded and coordinated by Iran's security services, the IRGC and MOIS (Ministry of Intelligence and Security), acting on orders from the highest levels of the regime in Tehran.[24]

Organizational blame was not placed solely on Saudi Hizballah's shoulders until they were indicted by the US Department of Justice five years later in June 2001.[25] Iran's strategy of creating ambiguity worked. Evidence against Iran and Saudi Hizballah was not expedient, was inconclusive and there was still no solid link between the two, thus making it more difficult to formulate any type of retaliation by the United States.

Marginalizing Enemy Neutrality
to Solidify the State's Position

Iran prefers to face the Unites States on an asymmetric battlefield, where material and technological advantages do not necessarily translate into success. To do this it must engage the United States on the periphery rather than on its own soil in open conflict. When the United States chooses to send its military forces to a foreign land, the local population may perceive US forces as liberators, as an intervening force, or as just another faction involved in a civil strife. The people directly affected by the fighting have the greatest stake in the conflict. The new *US Army/ Marine Corps Counterinsurgency Field Manual* reiterates this by explaining that legitimacy is best defined by the host population, not the international community or the intervening powers.[26]

In order to turn the local population against the United States and in favor of the influence of the militants and terrorists being sponsored by the state, Iran must make the United States appear to favor a certain faction. "Perception is the key that turns the population's neutrality into active acceptance. This competition is decidedly easier where the adversary . . . is an outsider and easily identifiable."[27] The faction favored by the United States could be the host country government or any of a number of warring militias in an area where the state does not hold a monopoly on power and coercion.

When the United States first sent peacekeepers to Lebanon in 1982, the war-weary local population welcomed them. However, due to events throughout 1982 and 1983, the United States lost its neutrality in the eyes of the local Lebanese people.

After high-level involvement by the US government and ten days of shuttle diplomacy by Secretary of State George Shultz, an agreement was reached that was supposed to end the state of war between Israel and Lebanon. The agreement, which would never be ratified due to strong Syrian opposition, was signed on 17 May 1983.[28] On 4 September 1983, Israel withdrew its forces from the Shouf Mountains in Lebanon in accordance with this accord. This move left a power vacuum in the area and led to increased fighting between the remaining factions. Israel's departure removed the last restraints between the Druze and Christians fighting for control of the high ground overlooking the US Marine encampment at the Beirut International Airport. The Druze and AMAL were pounding the Christians and pushing them out of much of their mountain turf. Once the Christians were pushed out of the mountains, the gateway to Beirut was opened except for the town of Souk al-Gharb. The Christians had to abandon the high ground in order to reinforce this town. The marines were now potentially exposed to Druze artillery.

The White House believed that the fall of Souk al-Gharb would spell the end of the Lebanese government. The Lebanese Army played to this and told the Americans that they were in danger of losing control of that vital position and pleaded for help. The Lebanese Army's commander, Brigadier Ibrahim Tannous claimed that the Iranians and Palestinians were also involved in the onslaught and that the government was in danger of collapse.[29] On 12 September the White House ordered US forces to come to the aid of the Christians. Marine Commander Colonel Geraghty resisted pressure from Reagan Administration Special Envoy Robert McFarlane to come to the Christians aid. He believed that helping the Christians at this point would not assure the safety of the Marines, nor would it do much to help the besieged Christians. The fall of Souk al-Gharb would not endanger the Marines any more than they already were. He believed that since the Druze already controlled the high ground by this point, there wasn't much that could be done to prevent the Druze from obliterating the Marines.[30]

The US Ambassador's residence came under fire, increasing the pressure on Colonel Geraghty. Finally, on 29 September, he relented. The United States shelled Syrian, Palestinian, and Druze positions for six days from the *USS John Rogers* and the *USS Virginia* offshore.[31] In the eyes of the factions fighting in Beirut this cost the United States its neutrality and relegated them to the position of just another tribal militia allied to the Lebanese government and its Christian President, Amin Gemayel. Since the Lebanese Army, led by a Maronite, was seen by the population of Lebanon as just another militia, the United States would find itself supporting a faction in a confusing conflict. The Lebanese believed the United States overstepped its boundary by the shelling of Druze and Syrian targets on the Shouf Mountains. This turned the US Marines into an "international militia" and thus subject to the lawlessness of the tribal war. This loss of neutrality made it easier for Iran to recruit local Shia Lebanese to join the fight against the United States and Israel.

Notes

1. Uri Ra'anan, Robert L. Pfaltzgraff, Jr., Richard H. Schultz, Ernst Halperin, and Igor Lukes, *Hydra of Carnage; International Linkages of Terrorism, The Witnesses Speak* (Lexington, Massachusetts: Lexington Books, 1986) 6-7.

2. Hala Jaber, *Hezbollah; Born With a Vengeance* (New York: Columbia University Press, 1997) 113.

3. "Islamism in Lebanon: A guide," *Al Mashriq*, September 1997, URL:,http://almashriq.hiof.no/lebanon/300/320/324.2/islamism/shia-islam-leb.html >, accessed 4 December 2004 (Hereafter cited as Islamism in Lebanon).

4. Brian A. Jackson, John C. Baker, Kim Cragin, John Parachini, Horacio R. Trujillo, and Peter Chalk, *Aptitude For Destruction; Volume 2, Case Studies of Organizational Learning in Five Terrorist Groups* (Santa Monica, Ca.: RAND Corporation, 2005) 42.

5. Thomas W. Shreeve, Col (USMCR), *Experiences To Go: Teaching With Intelligence Case Studies; Discussion Paper Number Twelve* (Washington D.C.: Joint Military Intelligence College, 2004) 32.

6. *The Beirut Memorial Online*, "Remarks by the Commandant of the Marine Corps to the Senate Armed Services Committee, 31 October 1983," URL: < http://www.beirut-memorial.org/history/kelley.html >, accessed 2 August 2009.

7. Tom Diaz and Barbara Newman, *Lightning Out of Lebanon; Hezbollah Terrorists on American Soil* (New York: Ballantine Books, 2005) 55-56.

8. Diaz and Newman, 58.

9. Jaber, 54.

10. Jaber, 82-83.

11. Diaz and Newman, 33-35.

12. Ra'anan, 140-141.

13. Jaber, 83.

14. Amal Saad-Ghorayeb, *Hizbu'llah: Politics and Religion* (London: Pluto Press, 2002) 6.

15. Shahram Chubin, *Whither Iran? Reform, Domestic Politics and National Security* (London: Oxford University Press, 2002) 89.

16. Saad-Ghorayeb, 94.

17. Saad-Ghorayeb, 95.

18. Jaber, 139.

19. Jaber, 99.

20. Sundri Khalsa, *Forecasting Terrorism; Indicators and Proven Analytic Techniques* (Lanham, Maryland: The Scarecrow Press, 2004) 76.

21. "Islamism in Lebanon: A guide," *Al Mashriq*, September 1997, URL: http://almashriq.hiof.no/lebanon/300/320/324.2/islamism/shia-islam-leb. html >, accessed 4 December 2004 (Hereafter cited as Islamism in Lebanon).

22. Diaz and Newman, 190-191.

23. *The 9/11 Commission Report: Final Report of the National Commission on Terrorist Attacks Upon the United States* (New York: W.W. Norton and Company, 2004) 60.

24. Richard L. Russell, "Iran in Iraq's Shadow: Dealing with Tehran's Nuclear Weapons Bid," *Parameters*, XXXIV, 3 (Autumn 2004): 31, 43.

25. "9/11 Panel Links Al Qaeda, Iran," *washingtonpost.com*, 26 June 2004, URL: <www.washingtonpost.com/ac2/wp-dyn/A6581-2004Jun25>, accessed 15 October 2004.

26. *The U.S. Army/Marine Corps Counterinsurgency Field Manual* (Chicago: The University of Chicago Press, 2007) 38.

27. Frank G. Hoffman, "Neo-Classical Counterinsurgency?" *Parameters*, XXXVII (Summer 2007): 83.

28. *The Official Lebanese Forces Website*, "May 17 Agreement," URL< http://www.lebanese-forces.org/lebanon/agreements/may17.htm>, accessed 3 August 2009.

29. Jaber, 79.

30. Richard A. Gabriel, *Military Incompetence; Why the American Military Doesn't Win* (Hill and Wang, 1986) 128-130.

31. Thomas L. Friedman, *From Beirut to Jerusalem* (New York: Random House, 1989) 200.

Chapter 4

Maintenance

Once the surrogate group has been created, there are certain things the state sponsor must do to ensure it will survive adversity and continue to be productive. For instance, Hizballah as an organization has thrived since 1982. It has grown, expanded, and adapted to its changing environment while retaining its core beliefs. None of this would have been possible without demonstrated successes; Iran and Hizballah's flexibility with regards to allies; popular support; and an information apparatus.

It is important for Iran with regards to its regional operational abilities to maintain some influence over Hizballah. Their affiliation with a coherent military organization in southern Lebanon provides Iran with valuable political leverage in the Arab world. Hizballah has provided and still provides Iran with a defense against a direct Israeli or American attack as a possible tool for retaliation.[1] This relationship also provides Iran leverage on the Arab "street." It shows the Arab and Muslim world that Iran is a state that is willing to strike at their common enemies, namely Israel and to an extent at the United States as Israel's ally. In Arab and Muslim eyes, due to their activity against Israeli occupation in Lebanon, Iran looks more like a supporter of "freedom fighters" than a supporter of terrorists.[2]

Enemy Casualties a Sign of Success

Iran and Hizballah are fighting a war of attrition against the Unites States. Both are trying to erode the will of the American people to fight in the Middle East. Iran and Hizballah seek to achieve this by causing the

American public to become disenchanted with the US government's Middle East policies. The more Americans killed in the Middle East, the more heated the debate becomes pressuring the US government to withdraw from the region. But America does not need to suffer mass casualties for Iran and Hizballah to achieve their intermediate range goals. Hizballah no longer actively targets Americans as they did in the 1980s. They are helping their cause by creating a perpetually hostile environment in hopes of driving the United States out of this area.

A horrific terrorist attack could tip the scales in favor of the terrorists. After the bombing of the Marine barracks in 1983, the US Marine contingent evacuated Beirut and moved to ships offshore.

> By effectively using mass, maneuver, economy of force, unity of command, security, surprise, and simplicity, a single terrorist "overcame the theoretical military advantage of a Marine amphibious unit supported by aircraft carriers, a battleship and the nation's combined intelligence capability to gain a major political victory."[3]

This was viewed by militants fighting in the conflict as a sign of US weakness, and supported Iran's ultimate goal of kicking the United States out of the region. The US reaction to a horrific terrorist attack by Islamist militants was seen as an expression of fear and weakness rather than moderation, and encouraged hope among Islamist militants that they would eventually triumph.[4]

Willingness to Work With Other Groups

Iran has shown a willingness to work with groups outside the Shia sect of Islam to achieve its objectives. Hizballah also has not been prejudiced against non-Shiites. They have been able to galvanize support from Iran and Syria because of their unified antagonism towards Israel. While Iran is dominated by hard-line Shia clerics, and Syria is ruled by Alawites and has a majority Sunni population, the conflict that has played out in Lebanon has served to consolidate these countries' support for Hizballah.[5]

According to Islamic scholars, Islam is a cultural, political, and intellectual expression transcending borders.[6] In general, Muslims bear a religious, legal responsibility towards their fellow Muslims, regardless of sect or geographical location. It demands the subordination of racial, tribal, and kinship affiliations. Iran and Hizballah officially reject the classification of Islam into national categories or classifications along racial lines.[7]

The American mindset that Shiites will not work with Sunnis due to a deep philosophical rift is strong. While this schism does exist, it is not as pronounced as Westerners think. According to the Palestinian Islamic Jihad, a Sunni movement, this schism is "an integral part of the world of Islam and consider existing controversies as marginal."[8] Iran has shown that it is willing to work with groups that do not necessarily share its particular Islamic beliefs.

> [T]he eastern Arab world has seen the odd spectacle of Sunni and Shiite extremists occasionally cooperating in the struggle against the infidels while continuing their internal struggle against one another . . . although the rift between the Sunnis and the Shiites is significant, Iran's involvement has rendered it less important than the divide between both of them and their non-Arab, non-Muslim enemies.[9]

The following are some examples of how Hizballah, a Shia-dominated organization, and Iran, a Shia theocracy, have cooperated with and at times supported Sunni-dominated terrorist groups. In 1991, the Iranian Pasdaran opened training bases in the Bekaa Valley for the newly formed Saudi Hizballah group, an offshoot of Hizballah. They provided funding, training, and passports.[10] That same year, informal agreements were made between Iranian elements in the Sudan at the time and al-Qaeda to provide support and training for al-Qaeda actions against the United States and Israel. In 1993, al-Qaeda representatives traveled to Iran and to Hizballah training camps in the Bekaa Valley to obtain training in explosives, intelligence gathering, and security.[11] In fact, Spain's top anti-terror judge Baltasar Garzon alleged, "al Qaeda had a 'board of managers' operating in Iran."[12] Reporting at the time indicated a multitude of contacts between Iran, Saudi Hizballah, and al-Qaeda in the early 1990s. Iran was helping al-Qaeda members relocate to Lebanon. Further, al-Qaeda representatives traveled to Iran and Hizballah training camps in Lebanon.[13]

Iran also was harboring Afghan fugitives fleeing Operation Enduring Freedom (OEF) in Afghanistan (a predominantly Sunni populated country). Iran has reportedly provided various types of training to Jaish Ansar as-Sunna, formerly Ansar al-Islam (AI). AI was a Kurdish group operating in Northern Iraq that absorbed Arab Afghan veterans and

Pashtuns (possibly Taliban from Afghanistan) that were fleeing OEF and sought refuge among the Kurds along the northern Iran/Iraq border.[14]

In October 2000, al-Qaeda attacked the *USS Cole* in the Port of Aden, Yemen. Between that time and the attack on the United States by al-Qaeda on 11 September 2001, there was increased cooperation between Iran, Hizballah, and al-Qaeda. Immediately following the attack on the *USS Cole*, Iranian officials approached al-Qaeda leadership and proposed a collaborative relationship in future attacks against the United States. However, al-Qaeda's leader Usama bin Laden (UBL) turned down the proposal so as not to alienate his Sunni, Saudi supporters.[15] Reporting also indicated meetings between bin Laden and IJO leader Imad Mughniyah.[16]

Between October 2000 and February 2001, eight of the future "muscle" hijackers from the 11 September attack traveled through Iran. Iranian officials issued specific orders to its border guards not to stamp the passports of Saudi terrorists traveling from al-Qaeda training camps through Iran. This was done because Iranian officials believed a Saudi passport with a Pakistani stamp on it would be confiscated upon that person's return to Saudi Arabia.[17]

Also in October 2000, shortly after the Israelis pulled out of Southern Lebanon, the current Palestinian Intifadah began. Hizballah reacted strongly and

> was quick to increase its level of cooperation with Palestinian rejectionists through direct training combined with logistical and operational support. Hizballah also put forth a significant effort towards establishing an independent terrorist and intelligence infrastructure inside both the Palestinian Authority and Israel. On the military front, the organization continued its cross-border attacks against Israeli forces in the Shebaa Farms area and expanded its arsenal of weaponry, acquiring rockets and missiles capable of reaching a greater number of Israeli targets.[18]

The Palestinian rejectionists mentioned above included Fatah, HAMAS, Palestinian Islamic Jihad, and other Palestinian security services. "Since the outbreak of the al Aqsa intifada in October 2000, Hezbollah [sic] has provided guerrilla training, bomb-building expertise, propaganda, tactical tips to HAMAS, Palestinian Islamic Jihad, and other anti-Israeli groups."[19] They have done this probably with Iranian and Syrian encouragement and at least tolerance of the Lebanese government.[20]

Hizballah, Iran, and Palestinian groups have cooperated in attempts at smuggling operations. An example of this was the *Karine-A* smuggling operation that was thwarted by Israel in January 2002. Iran and Hizballah were attempting to smuggle fifty tons of illegal weaponry aboard the freighter to the Palestinian Authority via the Red Sea when Israeli forces seized the ship carrying the weapons.[21] Another example was the arrest by the Israeli Navy of Hizballah explosives expert Hamad Muslam Musa Abu Amra. In May 2003 he was aboard the *Abu Hassan* headed for Gaza. Along with Amra, the Israelis seized explosives and bomb making materials.[22]

The Palestinian Islamic Jihad (PIJ) movement was started in Gaza, Israel in the 1970s. The Iran/PIJ relationship was enhanced by the deportation of the PIJ's leader, Fathi Shqaqi in 1988 to Lebanon. The PIJ headquarters were subsequently moved to Damascus, Syria and engaged in direct contacts with Iran through the Iranian Embassies in Beirut and Damascus. Iran supplied the PIJ with political, financial, and military assistance through the IRGC and Hizballah. The PIJ had been transformed into an organization similar in philosophy and structure to Hizballah. There were also regular political meetings between Hizballah Secretary General Nasrallah and Shqaqi.[23]

HAMAS was established in 1988 as the militant wing of the Muslim Brotherhood in Palestine. In 1990, HAMAS opened a permanent representation in Tehran. The political leaders of Hizballah and HAMAS met regularly in Lebanon. Iran invited a HAMAS delegation to Tehran in October 1992, after which Iran pledged support with money and access to training sites in Iran, Lebanon, and the Sudan. HAMAS received money through the Iranian Embassy in Jordan.[24] Further cooperation resulted from the December 1992 kidnapping of an IDF soldier by HAMAS. Israel retaliated by deporting 415 HAMAS members to southern Lebanon bringing more HAMAS members and leaders into Hizballah territory.[25]

Cooperation between Hizballah and Palestinian groups has not been hidden. Rather, it has been publicly acknowledged. On 21 April 2002, Hizballah official Mohammed Raab "acknowledged that Hezbollah [sic] provides Palestinians with military intelligence and suggestions for stockpiling supplies, trench building, and destroying tanks." In March 2004, Hizballah and HAMAS signed an agreement to increase joint efforts to mount attacks against Israel. And later in 2004, Hizballah leader Sheik Sayyed Hassan Nasrallah, while not specifically identifying the group, publicly acknowledged that Hizballah provided covert assistance to Palestinian militants.[26]

Iran and Hizballah had also increased activity with HAMAS to recruit Israeli Arabs and were attempting to establish cells in Israel to carry out espionage and terrorist activity.[27] In a March 1995 report published by al-Watan al-Arabi, a weekly publication in Paris, "Iran together with Hizbullah [sic], Islamic Jihad, HAMAS and other radical Islamic movements have been making special efforts to recruit young Muslims."[28]

Nurturing of Popular Support Through Special Programs

In order to nurture popular support so the surrogate organization can expand its membership over time, the group that originally was dedicated to achieving its goals solely through violence must create social programs in order to gain favor in the eyes of the local population. It can be expected that the area in conflict will be war-weary and deprived of basic social services after years of fighting. The surrogate groups can foster local popular support by providing services with the help of outside funding the government or occupying force is no longer able to provide. The government in power may also be unwilling to support these social services due to corruption, nepotism, and/or sectarianism. It also helps the state sponsor and its terrorist surrogate group to gain a broader support base when the social assistance is used to cross the cultural, ethnic, and religious boundaries and can reach out to all people affected by the conflict.

The state sponsor can contribute to this financial and social support either overtly or clandestinely. Of course the state sponsor will get more credit from the local population if the people know who is donating the funds and services. Either way, the connections between the state sponsor and the surrogate group should still remain hidden because of the expected continuation of violent cooperation between the state sponsor and the factions of the organization perpetrating terrorist acts. This social assistance can come from many institutions.

> With Iran's generous assistance, it [Hizballah] established a network of educational and cultural institutions, and also health and social welfare services. The latter included an Islamic health authority that operated pharmacies, clinics, and even hospitals. . . . The organization

also established a construction company that not only built houses, mosques and schools, but also paved roads and even supplied water to Shi'ite [sic] villages . . . maintained a Martyrs' Fund which provided assistance to thousands of families.[29]

Hizballah has tasked several of its organizations with the sole responsibility of building this kind of social network of support for the people it wishes to recruit and persuade. Their unit called the Campaign for Reconstruction Institution repairs homes damaged by IDF air strikes and bulldozers. The Martyrs' Foundation is responsible for aiding widows and children of their martyrs (Hizballah's description), and the Resupply Committee provides relief to the poor.[30]

Nurturing of Popular Support Through Political Activity

The organization must also become involved in the burgeoning political process if it wishes to be active after the violence stops and peace ensues. The state sponsor of a terrorist group will want the organization it has spent time, effort, and money on—and has assumed great risk in creating—to morph into a legitimate organization that can operate and grow outside the theater of war. The fear is that the organization employing resistance, insurgency, or terrorism will lose its relevancy when the conflict ends, no matter what form of government comes to power or which faction rules. In order for such an organization to achieve longevity, it must prepare for the peace. The state will want its surrogates, through the organization created, to be active in the new government that takes form after the conflict ends. Therefore, the state must ensure the organization gets involved in the political system as early as possible without compromising its ideological fervor. This entails a great deal of tolerance on the part of the state sponsor, as the surrogate will at times act in its own self interest as it matures.

With the civil war drawing to a close in 1990, the dominance of the militias was being threatened and a new era of political cooperation was emerging. The Taif Accord of 1989 was proposed to address the political imbalance in the current Lebanese system. Hizballah saw this more as a continuation of the status quo. However, they did realize that if they did not get involved in the rapidly evolving political situation they could end up being obsolete and isolated. With encouragement from Syria and Iran,

Hizballah dropped its earlier objections to participating in Lebanese politics and began their integration into the democratic process.[31]

Hizballah's popularity in Lebanon showed during its integration into Lebanese politics. In the parliamentary elections of 1992, after ten years of armed struggle Hizballah won 12 of the 128 seats to the national parliament. Eight of those seats were to Hizballah party members; four were to non-Shia supporters. Four years later, Hizballah won nine seats and achieved legitimization of its Islamic Resistance activity against the Israeli Defense Force from the Lebanese government. In 1998, in the first municipal elections in thirty-five years, Hizballah won almost half of all municipal council seats in the South, the overwhelming majority of seats in the Bekaa Valley, and all of the seats for the Shia districts in the southern suburbs of Beirut.[32]

While it can be argued that Hizballah's military capabilities are superior to those of the Lebanese army's, they have chosen to work within the current government framework rather than attempting to seize power through a violent overthrow.[33] They have been able to garner a wide base of support in a very diverse Lebanese society by abandoning their initial goal of establishing an Islamic Republic in Lebanon. Hizballah deemed the creation of an Islamic state as unfeasible and has demonstrated a willingness to work within the current system. They have been able to balance their intellectual commitment to the Velayat-e Faqih, or the infallibility of a supreme Islamic leader, as is used in Iran, with their allegiance to the Lebanese state.[34] Hizballah has come to accept that the notion of creating an Islamic Republic is too much of a utopia to merit serious political debate or to be considered a realizable political goal in such a diverse country as Lebanon.[35]

A document written by Hizballah presented to the al-Manar television station (Hizballah's TV station) explains its stated political intentions for Lebanon and the platform its candidates run under:

> We will seek with all carefulness that the Lebanese people with all its sects, categories and individuals, remain the Resistance's embracer and base from which it derives strength and presence. The sought-after liberation—Allah willing—will only be a gift to all Lebanese and a major contribution in constructing a country with complete sovereignty and a state of consideration and estimation in the arena of regional and international conflict. . . . Achieving justice and equality among the Lebanese is considered one of the main bases for establish-

ing a stable dignified and prosperous country in which all of the Lebanese engage in the process of construction with drive and solidarity under equality of opportunities, equality of all, individuals, classes and areas, in rights and duties, whether political, economical or social . . . Abolishing political sectarianism that represents the center of the essential flaw in the formula of the Lebanese political system and its social structure . . . A just and balanced electoral system that treats all the Lebanese evenhandedly . . . Establishing real political institutions that can not be summarized in individuals.[36]

Creation of an Information Apparatus to Disseminate Message

Due to the prowess of the international media, the local population involved in a conflict as well as the world at large will get information of the situation on the ground one way or another. An information campaign broadcast through many different media forms can disseminate the message that the state sponsor wants the local populace and the world to hear. If the state sponsor and the organization have an information apparatus that is trusted by the local populace they can transmit the message they have designed for the people.

The availability of a multitude of media has been a force multiplier for the militarily weaker combatant in modern insurgencies and terror campaigns. It has enhanced the manner by which "adversaries acquire and disseminate strategic intelligence, recruit, rehearse, and promote their cause." Modern media can reach international supporters and sympathizers more readily thus helping the combatants reliant on outside support to continue tapping the pipeline of foreign assistance essential to carrying on their fight.[37]

Hizballah has gotten its information out by creating an information apparatus capable of broadcasting propaganda through radio stations, publications, a television station, and the Internet. Hizballah's media responses to specific incidents demonstrate "how the group has become skilled at framing key episodes of political violence against the backdrop of historical themes that resonate with the group's domestic and regional constituencies."[38] Because of its knowledge of the local history and culture, Iran and Hizballah have been able to fight a successful information war. "Certainly, Hizballah waged its own effective propaganda campaign, using press, radio and television stations and even Internet web sites."[39] In the early years of Hizballah's propaganda campaign, they relied on journals to deliver their messages. Their first journal, *Al Ahd*, was launched on 13 June 1984[40] and was soon followed by other weekly journals, three radio stations, and print media through many of the group's websites, providing a convergent platform to what was already a robust media presence.[41]

One of Hizballah's primary means of media exploitation is their television station, al-Manar. Al-Manar began broadcasting from the Syrian-controlled Bekaa Valley region of southeastern Lebanon on 3 June 1991. They grew from a small, local station that serviced only parts of Beirut to a regional broadcaster. After switching to satellite broadcasting in 2000, they became a global television station able to reach new audiences worldwide.[42] Al-Manar produces propaganda videos of Hizballah operations and military parades. They also produce speeches given by Sheik Fadlallah and Secretary General Nasrallah.[43] Their programs and websites honor the "martyrs" who have tried to kill Israelis. Their most popular program, launched in the fall of 2003, is a game show called "The Mission." On this show:

> Contestants are given a monetary prize incentive to answer questions based on Hezbollah [sic] assertions about purported Israeli atrocities, alleged historic evils of Jews, American and European wickedness, names of terrorist martyrs and the like. Correct answers earn contestants points and move them on a map closer to Jerusalem. The first to reach 60 points lands on the holy city and is awarded five million Lebanese pounds (about $3,000) while a popular Hezbollah [sic] rally song plays.[44]

The most recent example of Hizballah's media campaign prowess is the 2006 war with Israel. By launching Katyusha rockets from holy sites and schools in southern Lebanon, Hizballah virtually ensured that Israel would retaliate and inflict civilian casualties since Israel was so reliant in that conflict on air strikes. While using innocent civilians as human shields is deplorable and cowardly, modern insurgents exploit this damage through choreographed images and stories to produce their desired effect.[45] Israel had expected the shock of Hizballah using schools and mosques as cover to turn the Lebanese population against Hizballah for recklessly using their innocent citizens as cannon fodder. However, rather than mobilizing the population against Hizballah, the collateral damage as exploited by media outlets sympathetic to Hizballah seemed to have had the opposite effect. It rallied and recruited sympathizers to Hizballah's side in the fight against Israel.[46]

Figure 1. How to Create a Surrogate Terrorist Organization

1. **Existence of an Area Under Conflict**
   Civil War or Foreign Intervention
   The State's Support of One Side
2. **Creation of the Surrogate Group**
   Infiltration by State Agents
   Possible Need for Cooperation From a Third Country
   Use of Existing Local Leaders
   Use of Existing Local Fighters
   Formation of an Umbrella Group
   Organization of the Group
   Training of and Equipping the Group
   Funding of the Group
   Legitimacy Gained Through Resistance
3. **Creation of Ambiguity to Avoid Responsibility/Blame**
   Operation Under Aliases
   Denial of Involvement and the Involvement of the Surrogate
   Creation, Working With, and Funding Other Groups
   Marginalizing Enemy Neutrality to Solidify the State's Position
4. **Maintenance**
   Enemy Casualties a Sign of Success
   Willingness to Work With Other Groups
   Nurturing of Popular Support Through Special Programs
   Nurturing of Popular Support Through Political Activity
   Creation of an Information Apparatus to Disseminate Message

Notes

1. Ali M. Ansari, *Iran Under Ahmadinejad: The Politics of Confrontation* (The International Institute for Strategic Studies, Adelphi Paper 393, London: Routledge, 2007) 65.
2. Anthony H. Cordesman, "Iran's Support of the Hezbollah in Lebanon," (*Center for Strategic and International Studies: Arleigh A. Burke Chair in Strategy*, Washington DC, 15 July 2006) 10.
3. Donald J. Hanle, *Terrorism: The Newest Face of Warfare* (New York: Pergamon-Brassey's International Defense Publishing, Inc., 1989), 157.
4. Bernard Lewis, "Free at Last? The Arab World in the Twenty-first Century," *Foreign Affairs*, 88, 2, (March/April 2009): 78.
5. Sarah E. Kreps, "The 2006 Lebanon War: Lessons Learned," *Parameters*, XXXVII, 1 (Spring 2007): 80.
6. Amal Saad-Ghorayeb, *Hizbu'llah: Politics and Religion* (London: Pluto Press, 2002) 75-77.
7. Ibid.
8. "The Terrorist Connection-Iran, The Islamic Jihad and HAMAS," *Federation of American Scientists*, May 1995, URL: < http://www.fas.org/irp/world/para/docs/950500.htm >, accessed 21 August 2004.
9. Lewis, 85-86.
10. Robert Baer, *See No Evil* (New York: Crown Publishers, 2002) 250.
11. *The 9/11 Commission Report: Final Report of the National Commission on Terrorist Attacks Upon the United States* (New York: W.W. Norton and Company, 2004) 91-93.
12. "9/11 Commission to implicate Iran," *Daily Times-Site Edition*, 18 July 2004, URL: < http://www.dailytimes.com.pk/story_18-7-2004 > accessed 15 October 2004.
13. "9/11 Panel Links Al Qaeda, Iran," *washingtonpost.com*, 26 June 2004, URL: < www.washingtonpost.com/ac2/wp-dyn/A6581-2004Jun25 >, accessed 15 October 2004.
14. Daniel Williams, "Italy Targeted By Recruiters For Terrorists," *Washington Post*, online ed., 17 December 2003, URL: < http:www.washington post.com/ac2/wp-dyn/A6172-2003Dec16?language >, accessed 5 January 2004.
15. 9/11 Commission to Implicate Iran.
16. "Al-Qaeda Members Reportedly Regrouping in Lebanon," *Interdisciplinary Center Herzliyn*, 3 February 2002, URL: < http://ict.org.il/spotlight/det.cfm?id=735 >, accessed 15 October 2004.
17. 9/11 Commission to Implicate Iran.
18. Fight on All Fronts: Hizballah, the War on Terror, and the War in Iraq," *Interdisciplinary Center Herzliyn*, 1 February 2004, URL: < www.ict.org.il/articles/articledet.cfm?articleid=510 >, accessed 15 October 2004.

19. Richard L. Russell, "Iran in Iraq's Shadow: Dealing with Tehran's Nuclear Weapons Bid," *Parameters*, XXXIV, 3 (Autumn 2004): 43.

20. Cordesman, "Lebanese Security and Hezbollah," 21.

21. Fight on All Fronts

22. Rachel Ehrenfeld, *Funding Evil; How Terrorism is Financed—and How to Stop It* (Los Angeles: Bonus Books, 2003) 131.

23. The Terrorist Connection.

24. The Terrorist Connection.

25. James J. F. Forest, *Teaching Terror; Strategic and Tactical Learning in the Terrorist World* (New York: Rowman and Littlefield Publishers, 2006) 196.

26. Anthony H. Cordesman, "Lebanese Security and Hezbollah," *Center for Strategic and International Studies: Arleigh A. Burke Chair in Strategy* (Washington DC, working draft revised 14 July 2006) 20-22.

27. "Hizballah, Bin Laden Seeking to Recruit 'Local Operatives' in Israel," *Interdisciplinary Center Herzliyn*, 26 June 2001, URL: < www.ict.org.id/ spotlightdet.cfm?id=629 >, accessed 15 October 2004.

28. The Terrorist Connection.

29. "Hizballah: New Course or Continued Warfare," *Middle East Review of International Affairs*, September 2000, 4, 3. URL: < http://meria.idc.ac.il/ journal/2000/issue3/jv4n3a3.html >, accessed 21 August 2004.

30. Brian A. Jackson, John C. Baker, Kim Cragin, John Parachini, Horacio R. Trujillo, and Peter Chalk, *Aptitude For Destruction; Volume 2, Case Studies of Organizational Learning in Five Terrorist Groups* (Santa Monica, Ca.: RAND Corporation, 2005) 51.

31. Hala Jaber, *Hezbollah; Born With a Vengeance* (New York: Columbia University Press, 1997) 71-73.

32. Saad-Ghorayeb, 46.

33. William K. Mooney, Jr., "Stabilizing Lebanon: Peacekeeping or Na-tion-Building," *Parameters*, XXXVII, 3 (Autumn 2007): 33.

34. Saad-Ghorayeb, 68.

35. Saad-Ghorayeb, 115.

36. "The Electoral Program of Hizbullah," *Al Mashriq*, 20 June 1997, URL: < http://almashriq.hiof.no/Lebanon/300/320/324.2/Hizballah/Hizballah-platform.html >, accessed 4 December 2004.

37. Frank G. Hoffman, "Neo-Classical Counterinsurgency?" *Parameters*, XXXVII (Summer 2007): 79-80.

38. *Arab Media & Society*, "Resistance beyond time and space: Hizbullah's media campaigns," URL: < http://www.arabmediasociety.com/?article=671 >, accessed 1 August 2009.

39. Hizballah, *Middle East Review of International Affairs*.

40. Jaber, 42.

41. *Arab Media & Society*.

42. Forest, 9.

43. Tom Diaz and Barbara Newman, *Lightning Out of Lebanon; Hezbollah Terrorists on American Soil* (New York: Ballantine Books, 2005) 185.

44. *Discoverthenetworks.org,* "Al-Manar (Television)," URL: < http://www. discoverthenetworks.org/groupProfile.asp?grpid=7045 >, accessed 1 August 2009.

45. Hoffman, *Parameters*, 82.

46. Kreps, *Parameters*, 72-79.

Chapter 5

Dealing With the Aftereffects

In order for the surrogate to remain a deniable arm of the state sponsor's foreign policy, the state sponsor must be tolerant of the surrogate's desire for a greater degree of autonomy as it matures. A surrogate will naturally pursue some of its own agenda. The state must maintain, support and be tolerant of the group over time. However, until or unless it is willing to openly support the organization and face the consequences, it must be willing to sever the relationship if it is no longer able to maintain a degree of separation and deniability.

After the surrogate organization has established itself and obtained some status in the region, the state controlling the group may find that the surrogate tries to break away to some extent and have more control over its own operations. One way for the surrogate to become more independent is to obtain alternative sources of finance so as to decrease its reliance on the original state sponsor. The surrogate group may also try to distance itself from the state in order to establish legitimacy in the eyes of the people. It may wish to exert its independence so as not to be viewed as a puppet of the state and compromise its maturing legitimacy.

The surrogate may also wish to increase its independence and autonomy to prevent it from being openly associated with the state sponsor. Should the state sponsor come under sanctions or condemnation from the international community, the surrogate organization can continue to operate.

Lack of Control

Because the relationship between the state sponsor and the surrogate must remain obscure, control by the state sponsor will become difficult. The sponsor must maintain a link with the terrorists to send the proper message to its intended adversary, but must be amorphous enough to deny the relationship. Complicating this is the fact that the organization grows and matures and develops a sufficient structure of its own. It loses its reliance on the state to provide it with advice and counseling on structure and management.

Iran has discovered that terrorist surrogates are easy to form but difficult to control and disband. The "militant clerics began to discover that cultivating and releasing revolutionary groups proved easier than controlling them."[1]

Iran's surrogate, Hizballah, operates today in countries around the world. They are especially active in the Tri-Border Area (TBA) of Argentina, Brazil, and Paraguay where they utilize local businesses, drug trafficking, and contraband networks. All of these activities raise the exposure of the group and threatens additional exposure of the Iran-Hizballah relationship.

Gaining Independence Through Alternate Sources of Finance

Any organization needs funding in one form or another to operate. The money must be raised either legally or illegally, either earned or donated. As the surrogate group becomes more autonomous it may seek outside funding, becoming less dependent on the original state sponsor.

Western intelligence sources estimate Hizballah's annual operational budget to be between $200 and $500 million.[2] In addition to funding, training, weapons, explosives, political, diplomatic, and organizational aid from Iran, and diplomatic, political, and logistical support from Syria, Hizballah finances its organization and operations in diversified ways.[3] Like other organizations it collects membership dues, sells publications, provides speaking tours, holds cultural and social events, solicits door-to-door, appeals to the wealthy members in its communities, and endorses regular donations from personal earnings. It also collects independent donations from Mosques and Islamic Centers.[4] They receive funds through charitable donations, business interests, and their Diasporas.

Diasporas are another structural component and source of external support. These globally dispersed communities, connected as never before by improved information and transportation technologies, comprise a growing category of external participants contributing significant resources and personnel to support respective communities.[5]

Hizballah has invested in enterprises and businesses in Lebanon. They have opened co-operative supermarkets in the Beirut suburbs and other areas of the country. They have entered the real estate market, they operate "bookshops, stationers, farms, fisheries, factories, and bakeries."[6] Hizballah also has official channels to raise funds. The Islamic Resistance Support Organization (IRSO) is the official fundraising arm of Hizballah's political party. It manages international fund raising efforts through Hizballah's Foreign Affairs Office in Beirut. According to the US Department of Treasury, Hizballah uses the IRSO to

> solicit donations in support of its terrorist activities . . . IRSO has identified itself to prospective donors as one and the same as Hizballah. Solicitation materials distributed by IRSO inform prospective donors that funds will be used to purchase sophisticated weapons and conduct operations. Indeed, donors can choose from a series of projects to contribute to, including supporting and equipping fighters and purchasing rockets and ammunition.[7]

Hizballah also has expanded efforts to receive support from external sources and has tapped into worldwide financial networks as well. These sources are especially difficult for their adversaries to target, as there is simply too much porosity in modern financial infrastructures. These financial institutions depend on the rapid movement of capital and the preservation of wealth and liquidity in virtual form.

Hizballah understands how to work the international financial network by hiding evidence that could alert most Western financial crime monitors. The group launders illicit funds through Middle Eastern banks to key individuals secretly engaged in terrorism, but only loosely associated with Hizballah. Iran and Hizballah use front companies to funnel money to Hizballah members. They fund terrorist activities through international companies that have been established by the Shiite international commercial elite, that are controlled by Hizballah leaders, and that recycle funds through Western banks.[8] However, transnational support networks, if properly targeted, constitute "the Achilles' heel of these networks."⁹ A disruption of these funds could place Hizballah further under the control of Iran.

While a large portion of funds procured by Hizballah are in the form of direct aid from Iran and from legal activity, a substantial amount of money is obtained illegally. They have the ability to draw resources from various financial resources such as regional drug and criminal networks. Hizballah has long engaged in drugs-for-cash deals, with operatives smuggling cocaine from Latin America to Europe and the Middle East.¹⁰ This illicit business generates tens of millions of dollars annually for Hizballah. Not only do they smuggle cocaine from Latin America, they also are involved in the production and trade of heroin and cocaine from areas in Lebanon under the nominal control of Hizballah and Syria. When Hizballah established itself in the Bekaa Valley in the early 1980s, it appropriated and increased the area's already ongoing production of hashish and heroin.¹¹

In the mid-1980s, Hizballah clerics began planting operatives and recruiting new members from among the large Muslim community of the Tri-Border Area (TBA) of Argentina, Brazil, and Paraguay. Iran originally saw this area as a location to build support for the Revolution. However, with the rise of Hizballah, they realized that they could use the Shia there more directly and began organizing Hizballah cells. This was done through the Ministry of Interior often operating within the Ministry of Culture and Islamic Guidance, which gave the program a softer façade.¹² This area's porous borders and unstable and corrupt governments gave Hizballah and other criminal organizations a complicit zone in which to operate.¹³ Their exploitation of the TBA as a source of funding outside of Iran is crucial. They are extensively using this area to raise funds to diminish their reliance on money from Tehran.¹⁴

Hizballah is involved in narcotics trafficking, smuggling, money laundering, and terrorist activity in the TBA. They have developed relationships with nacro-terrorist and drug trafficking organizations from Colombia, Peru, and Bolivia—including the Revolutionary Armed Forces of Colombia (FARC), the National Liberation Army (ELN) of Colombia, and the Sendero Luminoso (Shining Path) in Peru.¹⁵ An individual of note is Hizballah operative Assad Muhammad Barakat. Identified by the Paraguayan police as Hizballah's military chief in the TBA, Barakat is believed to have been involved in the 1994 bombing of the Jewish Community Center in Buenos Aires. The Argentinean police claimed that Barakat had distributed $60 million in Colombian-printed counterfeit dollars to his Hizballah bosses. An associate, Sobhi Mahmoud Fayad, who had been coordinating fund-raising operations with Barakat, is the brother of a high-ranking Hizballah official in Lebanon. It is estimated that he had moved more than $3.5 million to the ash-Shahid Association, an organization that Barakat had also sent money to.[16]

Hizballah receives financial support from charitable donations and extortion of Lebanese immigrants in the United States. This money comes mainly from cities with large Shia communities such as Detroit, New York, Boston, and Los Angeles. Any money received by Hizballah can be used for all facets of their operations, from social services to terrorism.[17]

An example of Hizballah illegal activity in the United States was the July 2000 cigarette smuggling scheme the FBI called Operation Smoke Screen. The Hizballah cell leader was Muhammad Youssef Hammoud. Hammoud was born on 25 September 1973 in the Bourj al-Barajneh neighborhood in southeast Beirut.[18] He was well connected to the Hizballah hierarchy in Lebanon and was reported to be close to Hizballah spiritual leader Fadlallah. He had received military training in Lebanon. The FBI had wiretaps of Hammoud speaking to Sheikh Abbas Harake, Hizballah's military commander in Beirut.

The cell was based in Charlotte, North Carolina. There they held regular Thursday night prayer meetings in which they would read messages containing directives for the members. These messages had been transmitted from a Hizballah official in Lebanon to Muhammad Hassan Dbouk, a Canadian colleague who was a reconnaissance and surveillance specialist believed to have worked for Hizballah's Security Chief and deadliest terrorist, Imad Mughniyah. The cell was exploiting the seventy-cent difference in the tax on cigarettes between North Carolina and Michigan. Each carload of cigarettes bought in North Carolina and illegally transported to Michigan would yield between $3,000 and $10,000. Over a year and a half of smuggling, until they were caught, the cell had generated an estimated $7.9 million.[19]

Hammoud's cell was not the only Hizballah group operating on US soil. Prior to Operation Smoke Screen, a Hizballah operative was arrested in July 1998 in Detroit trying to purchase $100,000 worth of thermal imaging gear. In September 2001, another Hizballah operative in Detroit was convicted of having shipped weapons and ammunition to Hizballah in Lebanon. The money obtained through criminal activity by these cells is sent to Lebanon to their Hizballah bosses in a number of different ways. The money is transferred using the *hawala* system, an informal form of banking common in the Middle East. The money is also wire transferred if the sums are less than $10,000. Cash is carried to Lebanon on individuals or shipped via courier companies.[20]

These criminal operatives that operated on US soil as well as cells that have yet to be discovered have the ability to move people across the borders and give them new identities. They have access to a constant flow of untraceable cash, military training, and a network of criminal contacts to get weapons.[21]

Desire to Distance Itself from the Sponsor to Establish Legitimacy

Hizballah has sought to overturn the once pervasive perception that it is an Iranian surrogate and is devoid of any national identity or loyalty towards its host, Lebanon. They recognize that this accusation takes legitimacy from the party. Hizballah has "publicly striven to harmonize its Islamic identity, of which its affiliation to the Islamic Republic and the concept of the Wilayat al-Faqih [sic] is an intrinsic part, with its national identity."[22] The intellectual bond between Iran and Hizballah is consecrated by the concepts of the Velayat-e Faqih, but not directed by it. This intellectual bond is stronger than all others, but must not be confused with a political bond. Hizballah claims that the Iranian state does not command its paramount loyalty; this is reserved for the Lebanese state. In a televised debate in 1996 on the Lebanese Broadcasting Company (LBC), a leading station founded and controlled by the Christian Lebanese Forces, Hizballah's Secretary General Nasrallah stressed this. He stated, "we are fighting on behalf of a people, a nation and a government."[23]

Notes

1. Sandra Mackey, *The Iranians* (New York: Penguin Group, 1998) 316.
2. Rachel Ehrenfeld, *Funding Evil; How Terrorism is Financed-and How to Stop It* (Los Angeles: Bonus Books, 2003) 124.
3. Anthony H. Cordesman, "Lebanese Security and Hezbollah," *Center for Strategic and International Studies: Arleigh A. Burke Chair in Strategy* (Washington DC, working draft revised 14 July 2006) 20.

4. Steven Metz, "The Ideology of Terrorist Foreign Policies in Libya and South Africa," *Conflict*, 7, 4, (Crane, Russak & Co., 1987): 379-401.

5. Frank G. Hoffman, "Neo-Classical Counterinsurgency?" *Parameters*, XXXVII (Summer 2007): 74.

6. Hala Jaber, *Hezbollah; Born With a Vengeance* (New York: Columbia University Press, 1997) 152.

7. *United States Department of the Treasury*, "Terrorism and Financial Intelligence, Key Issues, Protecting Charitable Organizations," URL < http://www.ustreas.gov/offices/enforcement/key-issues/protecting/charities_execorder_13224-i.shtml >, accessed 2 August 2009.

8. Ehrenfeld, 126.

9. Shawn Brimley, "Tentacles of Jihad: Targeting Transnational Support Networks," *Parameters*, XXXVI, 2 (Summer 2006): 31.

10. Julia Baunder, editor, *Drug Trafficking: Current Controversies* (New York: Greenhaven Press, 2008) 218.

11. Ehrenfeld, 143-145.

12. Tom Diaz and Barbara Newman, *Lightning Out of Lebanon; Hezbollah Terrorists on American Soil* (New York: Ballantine Books, 2005) 122.

13. Ehrenfeld, 145-146.

14. Metz, 379-401.

15. Ehrenfeld, 147.

16. Ehrenfeld, 150.

17. Ehrenfeld, 133.

18. Diaz and Newman, 7-9.

19. Ehrenfeld, 137-139.

20. Ehrenfeld, 142-143.

21. Ehrenfeld, 140.

22. Amal Saad-Ghorayeb, *Hizbu'llah: Politics and Religion* (London: Pluto Press, 2002) 82.

23. Jaber, 46.

Chapter 6

Surrogate Centers of Gravity That Can Be Exploited

Nineteenth Century Prussian soldier, military historian and theorist Karl von Clausewitz stated in his treatise, *On War*, that a center of gravity (COG) is "that point in the enemy's organism—military, political, social, etc.—at which, should he be defeated, or should he lose it, the whole structure of national power will collapse."[1] There are several centers of gravity in the state sponsor/surrogate group relationship that can be exploited. This type of relationship has some unique characteristics making it potentially vulnerable to hostile forces. First, in this relationship both the state sponsor and the surrogate may be forced to rely on other countries or non-state groups due to geography or necessity. Second, the surrogate militant or terrorist group that follows Mao's classic insurgency strategy is dependent on the local population. Third, as with any type of organization, leadership preservation is essential. Fourth, the need for secrecy to keep the relationship covert to the benefit of both the state sponsor and the surrogate is vital. And finally, Hizballah has physical structures in fixed locations that are vulnerable to military attack.

Dependence on Other Countries

In order for the state sponsor to get the needed funds and equipment to the terrorists or insurgents, as well as to infiltrate its own people into the area to provide guidance and training, it will often have to rely on other countries or non-state groups that are powerful in the area of the conflict. If the state sponsor does not share a border with the critical area of conflict, it will have to rely on others to control access to the area. Even if a shared border exists, the state may have to rely on powerful non-state groups operating along the often lawless border regions to exert influence in the area and assist in controlling the supply lines.

Iran supplies Hizballah with a significant amount of funding and equipment, spiritual guidance, logistics, and weapons. Iran also supplies military advisors and training within Iran and Lebanon. Hizballah in turn relies on Iran and Syria for protection from debilitating military strikes in an all-out military confrontation by making clear that the consequences would be a wider regional war. Its guerrilla forces are relatively weak compared to the military power of its enemies, namely the Unites States and the Israeli Defense Forces. These forces are also fairly easy to target when compared to its terror network.

Syria provides Hizballah with an overall strategic umbrella, with respect to military and political coordination and local pressure in Lebanon. Syria can pressure Beirut to give Hizballah free rein in Southern Lebanon because of Syria's hegemony over Lebanese internal affairs. Syria's involvement is therefore critical to Hizballah operating freely in Southern Lebanon.

Hizballah regards "Syrian support as vital for it to maintain an overt and sanctioned stance in Lebanon."[2] Syria allows a continuous supply of military equipment from Iran via a land route through Damascus. Iran is also allowed to use Damascus International Airport to transport material to Beirut International Airport en route to Hizballah bases.[3] Hizballah realizes it can only maintain a continued operational presence in Lebanon with Syria's compliance and therefore, in addition to allegiance to Iran, it must support Syrian politics as well.

The Need For Local Popular Support

This is where terrorists and insurgents differ. Control of a population is essential in order to establish an alternate political order under the classic insurgent model as practiced by Mao-inspired movements. Author Ralph Peters states that the "dividing line between a terrorist group and an insurgency lies between the inability of the former to attract mass support and the ability of an insurgent movement to mobilize the population whose cause they claim to represent."[4]

Modern insurgents utilizing terrorist tactics seek to create and sustain a perpetual state of chaos, disorder, and violence to push the ruling government or intervening force into capitulating. They do not, unlike classic insurgents, seek to conquer and hold territory and replace the existing structure with one of their own as they progress along Mao's insurgency model. They simply seek to drive the current powers out. Without the hierarchy in place and the popular support they cannot hope to create order out of the chaos in the near term. The establishment of an alternative form of government in line with their philosophy may be their ultimate goal, but without the mentioned support, they will not be able to supply the people with the necessary social services and bureaucratic mechanism that is needed from a modern government.

Support from the local populace allows terrorists and guerrilla operatives to slip in and out of the urban terrain. Without this support, these groups would be more vulnerable to opposition intelligence and military services. Hizballah may have looked like a modern insurgency whose only tactic was terror and only goal was to create chaos in Lebanon in the early 1980s. However, they have followed many of the phases of the classic insurgent model. The exception being that, along the way, instead of wresting territory away from the Lebanese government, they have chosen to replace the existing order with members of their own party to rule within the established structure.

Lebanese popular support was and is critical in giving Hizballah a base from which to operate and move freely. The Lebanese people credit Hizballah with forcing the United States to withdraw from Beirut in 1983 and forcing Israel to withdraw from Southern Lebanon in 2000. The people have rewarded Hizballah at the voting booths. This local support is an essential factor for their continued existence and its developing legitimacy.

Leadership Preservation

Hizballah's leadership preservation is essential in that a new leader may not be as pragmatic or as capable as Hassan Nasrallah. They have opted for a more loose and fluid structure as opposed to a more rigid one. This loose structure, similar to the clerical rule in Iran, revolves around the personal appeal of its religious leaders.[5] Hizballah needs to maintain an effective organizational structure governed by strong leaders such as Nasrallah, former IJO leader Mughniyah, and spiritual leader Fadlallah.

The Need to Keep the Relationship Secret

The maintenance of a secret relationship, or at least a deniable one, works to both Iran's and Hizballah's advantages. Iran needs to be able to continue to deny that they control the actions of Hizballah so as not to draw the full force of an Israeli or American retaliation. In order for Iran to sustain its surrogate as a valuable resource it must continue to covertly finance them through illegal activities and hidden funding. In order to continue to receive funding and equipment, Hizballah must maintain covert coordination with Lebanon, Syria, TBA elements, other terrorist organizations, and Iran's IRGC and MOIS.

Fixed Locations

Hizballah has used the cellular structure to carry out terrorist attacks against the United States and Israel. These cells have proven very difficult for military, law enforcement, and intelligence agencies to target. They have also followed a classic insurgency formula and have built up an impressive military with accompanying training facilities, weapons caches, and various support networks. These physical structures and fixed locations throughout the Bekaa Valley, southern Lebanon, and Beirut constitute a potential vulnerability for Hizballah. Michael Scheuer in his book *Through Our Enemies' Eyes* states that while "cruise missiles are nearly useless against al Qaeda's dispersed forces, they are a strong deterrent against nation-states and terrorist groups whose infrastructure is concentrated in a single state."[6]

Notes

1. Donald J. Hanle, *Terrorism: The Newest Face of Warfare* (New York: Pergamon-Brassey's International Defense Publishing, Inc., 1989), 37.

2. "Hizballah in the Firing Line," *Middle East Report OnLine*, 28 April 2002, URL: < http://www.merip.org/mero/mero042803.html >, accessed 17 September 2004.

3. Fight on All Fronts: Hizballah, the War on Terror, and the War in Iraq," *Interdisciplinary Center Herzliyn*, 1 February 2004, URL: <www.ict.org.il/articles/articledet.cfm?articleid=510>, accessed 15 October 2004.

4. Ralph Peters, *Wars of Blood and Faith: The Conflicts That Will Shape the Twenty-First Century* (Mechanicsburg, Pa: Stackpole Books, 2007) 7.

5. Hala Jaber, *Hezbollah; Born With a Vengeance* (New York: Columbia University Press, 1997) 63.

6. Michael Scheuer, *Through Our Enemies' Eyes; Osama bin Laden, Radical Islam, and the Future of America, Revised Edition* (Washington D.C.: Potomac Books, 2006) 196.

Chapter 7

Conclusion: What Aren't We Seeing But Should Be?

If Iran follows the model it used so successfully when creating Hizballah, then regional experts should see similar things happening in a country or region they suspect Iran is seeking to influence. In such an area, there may be evidence that Iran is following many of the steps and using techniques that proved successful in the past. However, in some cases there may be little or no evidence of this. Two things can explain this. One, the creation of a surrogate terrorist group is a process occurring over time. Because there is no evidence Iran is doing one of the steps may mean that it is not the time in the process to engage in that specific activity. Two, the creation of a surrogate terrorist group must be accomplished clandestinely. For this reason, the evidence to support this model may be forthcoming and/or may be hidden. Lack of evidence does not mean that evidence is lacking. Regional experts could use the model discussed in this book to create a list of indicators and warning signs to predict Iran's actions in a country or region that both the United States and Iran seek to influence.

The model created from this research shows many of the conditions, activities, and events necessary to create a state-sponsored group that utilizes terrorism during its creation to achieve its goals. While this group may morph over time to become a more legitimate organization in the interest of its state sponsor, during its creation in a time of conflict, its activities, intended to influence the situation in the country or region where it is located, will be heavily centered on terrorist and militant activity.

The 2003 US invasion of Iraq brought fears to the surface of members of the Iranian ruling elite of a US attempt to encircle Iran militarily. The signing of the recent US-Iraq defense pact was criticized in Iran as infringing on Iraqi sovereignty. This criticism may have masked Iran's fear that the pact would consolidate US power with that of Iran's neighbor.[1] The possibility of a US victory in Iraq was creating great anxiety in Iran. Many felt that it might be better if the United States were engaged in a prolonged conflict, one that would sap their energy and ambition for further conflict in the region, especially against Iran.[2]

Iranian President Ahmadinejad claimed the invasion of Iraq was a fatal mistake for the Americans. He believed that American power was frail and in decline and that this conflict would expose its true weaknesses. He saw this as an opportunity to further Iran's goals of pushing the United States out of the region while increasing Iran's dominance. Iran was, he felt, the ideal candidate to fill the vacuum left by the Americans when they inevitably departed.[3]

Iran's strategy in Iraq is two-fold. First, they wish to prevent the minority Sunnis from regaining power while providing broad support for the Iraqi Shia. Should a civil war ensue, Iran wants their fellow Shia to be in a stronger position than the Sunnis. Iran has established and maintains close ties with Iraqi Shia militias to accomplish their second goal: to resist American military presence.[4]

IRGC networks established in Iraq, both civil and military, were intended to allow Iran to influence the flow of events in their neighboring country. Their access to Iraqi society has been facilitated by extensive social networks linking Shia clerical families dating back generations. These close and personal relationships partnered with Iranian's intimate knowledge of the Iraqi landscape give Iranians a greater ability to maneuver around in the complex environment. Also, due to their success in Lebanon and the IRGC's success supporting Iran-friendly militias in Iraq during the 1980-88 war, they have institutional experience in quickly creating military, terrorist, political and social systems out of chaos.[5] General David Petraeus, the US Commanding General of the Multi-National Force-Iraq (MNF-I), stated in April 2008, that Iran continues to arm, train, organize, and direct "Special Groups" to serve Iran's interests and to fight a proxy war against Coalition forces and Iraqi state security forces if need be.[6]

During the creation of a surrogate terrorist group, there are a number of events and circumstances that have to take place. There are often gaps in intelligence collection in areas of conflict and chaos as well as areas controlled by hostile forces. Intelligence gaps are questions for which analysts lack evidence or have evidence of unknown information validity.[7] There are reasons for these gaps. Chief among them is that the creation of a surrogate terrorist group is a process occurring over time. Evidence to support this model may therefore be forthcoming only in the future. The following is speculation on what those gaps might be and areas that regional experts should focus on when trying to determine if Iran (or another state) is trying to form a surrogate terrorist organization in an attempt to influence events in a certain country or region.

1. It would be easier for Iran to coordinate support for the militants and terrorists in a country if the various groups were organized under a single umbrella group. Evidence will need to be sought of the IRGC, the Quds Force, and/or MOIS agents working closely with specific militant or terrorist groups.

2. In order for the surrogate to carry out terrorist operations, it must obtain the skills and expertise needed to be a successful terrorist group. Iran is a successful state sponsor of terrorism and has supported terrorists worldwide by providing training and weapons. Iran has terrorist training camps within its borders and supports camps in Lebanon. Terrorists will need to travel to Iran or Lebanon to train at these sites. Regional experts should look for insurgents traveling to and from Iran (and/or currently Lebanon) with Iran's assistance to train in these camps. If Iran does not wish to or is not able to help facilitate travel for these terrorists to the camps, its other option is to build and staff terrorist training camps in the country or region of interest or to take over existing facilities and provide Quds Force and/or MOIS personnel to train the terrorists.

3. The terrorist groups that Iran seeks to influence must also be funded. If Iran wishes to maintain plausible deniability with regards to its support for terrorism, the transfer of funds must be done covertly. Regional experts should look for

money being channeled to terrorist groups or individuals associated with them.

4. According to the model, the state sponsor will try to confuse
    and misdirect the intelligence gathering agencies of its en-
    emies. Militant and terrorist groups will quite possibly change
    names or operate under aliases when they claim responsibil-
    ity for terrorist activity. If there is a terrorist group being
    formed by Iran that is in the early stages of organization and
    development, it may not be inclined to claim acts of terror-
    ism in its own name. Regional experts should focus more on
    individuals and their relationships with Iranians, especially
    Quds Force and MOIS personnel, not the names of particu-
    lar organizations to draw the connections between Iran and
    the terrorist operators.

5. Another way Iran may increase the confusion and tension in
    a conflict area would be to put the US-led or international
    peace-keeping forces in a position favoring a certain group,
    or at least being viewed as having lost their neutrality. The
    other groups will not view the Americans as neutral and will
    have someone to focus their aggression against.

6. Iran must be willing to work with groups in addition to Shia
    Muslims if it hopes to achieve longevity with its surrogate
    terrorist groups in an area with a diverse culture. Iran has
    shown in the past that it is willing to work with groups out-
    side the Shia sect to achieve its objectives. Regional experts
    should look for groups connected to Iran that are showing a
    willingness to cross cultural lines. These terrorist groups will
    achieve greater long-term success in a diverse culture than
    groups that are unwilling to operate with groups or individu-
    als outside their own demographics.

7. Iran will want its surrogates, through the organization it cre-
    ates, to be important in the new government that takes form
    after the conflict ends. Therefore, the organization must get
    involved in the political system as early as possible without
    compromising its ideological fervor. Iran would actively sup-

port political activists sympathetic to their goals or those of the surrogate terrorist group. These candidates can be funded by Iran and made to appear as helping meet critical social needs of the local population. It is important to identify who these individuals are and expose their ties to Iran.

8. Lastly, the surrogate terrorist group will have to get its message out through an information apparatus. In order to create this medium, it will need funding and technological expertise that it may not already have. Regional experts should look for a terrorist group with ties to Iran that sets up a structure similar to what Hizballah has in order to broadcast its message and monitor any existing apparatus for messages that reinforce Iran's goals for the region.

Notes

1. Kenneth Katzman, "Iran's Activities and Influence in Iraq," *Congressional Research Service Report for Congress* (Library of Congress, Order Code RS22323, 17 September 2008) 6.

2. Ali M. Ansari, *Iran Under Ahmadinejad: The Politics of Confrontation* (The International Institute for Strategic Studies, Adelphi Paper 393, London: Routledge, 2007) 59.

3. Ansari, 58-59.

4. Gawdat Bahgat, "United States-Iranian Relations: The Terrorism Challenge," *Parameters*, XXXVIII, 4 (Winter 2008-09), 97.

5. Ansari, 60.

6. Kenneth Katzman, "Iran's Activities and Influence in Iraq," *Congressional Research Service Report for Congress* (Library of Congress, Order Code RS22323, 17 September 2008) 3.

7. Sundri Khalsa, *Forecasting Terrorism; Indicators and Proven Analytic Techniques* (Lanham, Maryland: The Scarecrow Press, 2004) 28.

Index

* Some Arabic words may be preceded by the participle ad, al, as, ash, etc. In such cases, the word is listed in the index according to the first letter of the following word.

About the Author

Stephen Kramer is an Intelligence Analyst for the US Government's Intelligence Community. He has also served as a Security Consultant in post-conflict areas of the world.

www.ingramcontent.com/pod-product-compliance
Lightning Source LLC
Chambersburg PA
CBHW021822270326
41932CB00007B/298